T0131503

Trait Reader

How to Accurately & Instinctively
Assess a Person or Situation Within 10
Seconds – An Invaluable Aid in Business
& Personal Decision-Making

DEBORAH JOHNSON

BALBOA.
PRESS
A DIVISION OF HAY HOUSE

Balboa Press books may be ordered through booksellers or by contacting:

Balboa Press
A Division of Hay House
1663 Liberty Drive
Bloomington, IN 47403
www.balboapress.com
1 (877) 407-4847

Because of the dynamic nature of the Internet, any web addresses or links contained in this book may have changed since publication and may no longer be valid. The views expressed in this work are solely those of the author and do not necessarily reflect the views of the publisher, and the publisher hereby disclaims any responsibility for them.

The author of this book does not dispense medical advice or prescribe the use of any technique as a form of treatment for physical, emotional, or medical problems without the advice of a physician, either directly or indirectly. The intent of the author is only to offer information of a general nature to help you in your quest for emotional and spiritual well-being. In the event you use any of the information in this book for yourself, which is your constitutional right, the author and the publisher assume no responsibility for your actions.

Any people depicted in stock imagery provided by Thinkstock are models, and such images are being used for illustrative purposes only. Certain stock imagery © Thinkstock.

Print information available on the last page.

ISBN: 978-1-5043-4792-1 (sc)
ISBN: 978-1-5043-4793-8 (e)

Balboa Press rev. date: 04/06/2016

CONTENTS

Introduction

PREFACE

My philosophy, insight, and practice has always been based on my ability to read between the lines; to use subliminal and semi-subliminal sensory awareness and association through names, words and actions to gain additional information and insight about someone or something.

The ability I use is already in all of us. It isn't a skill to be learned it is an instinctual power to be awakened. Trust in ourselves is paramount in all we do.

It is our social conditioning and generational passive control that has bred into us that element of self-doubt. It is this self-doubt that limits us.

We all emit energy that can be interpreted by others. Those around us can generally tell when we display extreme energy such as anger, happiness or sadness. People can surmise if something seems to be troubling us or worrying us even though we haven't uttered a single word. This form of awareness goes beyond body language and taps into what is the very essence of all of us – our energy.

What we emit energetically others perceive. What they display in turn we sense. We are comprised of so much more than our physical bodies and our physical presence. If we begin to recognize, appreciate, understand and utilize our own energy we will quickly come to realize that we have a powerful innate ability that, if used effectively, can take us far beyond our own expectations in all areas of our lives.

When we truly grasp the magnitude of our capabilities through the use of our own energy, will we be able to perceive on a much higher level. We will open up a whole new realm of awareness for ourselves.

Whether we do it consciously or subconsciously, we all emit subliminal vibrational messages to those around us such as what we emit through the power of prayer or well wishes to someone in crisis. We have the capacity to unite with others to create those incredibly moving emotions I am sure we have all experienced at large concerts, games, or mass celebrations when thousands come together. And just as we emit, we have the ability to receive this energy from others in the form of thoughts, feelings, ideas, words and actions. We have power far greater than what we realize if we think outside the box and understand what we are made of, and as a result of this, what we are capable of.

When we understand and learn how to utilize this dynamic of ourselves effectively, we will be able to intentionally recognize, interpret and upload subliminal information generated by others. This newfound awareness and ability will also add a new form of personal guidance and direction to our lives - simple in concept and practice, simple in execution, and profound in result.

Our energy is what makes us laugh, makes us cry, pulls at our heartstrings, drives us, inspires and motivates us. Our energy is our emotions, our thoughts, our feelings, our caring, our compassion, our actions, and our ideas. Our energy defines us.

It is this energy awareness and the possibilities we have with it that have motivated me to share what I do, how I do it, and how you can utilize your own natural senses to enrich all areas of your life immeasurably once you tap into it.

For the past twenty plus years I have worked one-on-one with thousands of individuals from all walks of life. My abilities have been used to give guidance and direction to CEO's and Executives of multi-million dollar organizations and to envision for those starting up an entrepreneurial endeavour. I have dealt with those seeking comfort and longing to connect with a departed loved one and I have helped those struggling through separations, depression, divorces, abusive relationships and financial strife. I have celebrated with my clients when they have overcome their obstacles, welcomed a newborn into their family or met that person of their dreams.

Yet all the work I do from giving visionary insight; to medium work with those who have passed; to corporate advice or employee placement, my work is all energy based. That is the beauty of energy, what we are made of, and who we are – there are no boundaries. Energy and the benefits of it are limitless as it is part and parcel of all of us. Therefore it applies to all we do.

I thank you for picking up the information I am sharing, and delving into an area of awareness still not totally understood by many, yet second-nature to me. These concepts will help shed some light and give you some tools and techniques that will be valuable to your life and the lives of those you touch. Since so much of what I will be covering is instinctual, you will find that the information within will automatically become part of your analytical processes.

Don't worry about 'right' and 'wrong'. When you learn how to listen to yourself and <u>trust</u> yourself again, you will never steer yourself wrong. Everything you do in your entire life will be pure value-add to you in some form when all is said and done.

Embrace your life. Expand your awareness. Come to understand, and then fully use, the ability you already possess.

FORWARD

Ushering the personable young twenty-two year old into my office, I indicated for him to take a seat. He was nicely groomed and seemed well spoken as we began the interview process. I noted he had held quite a number of positions for someone his age and length of time in the working world. He replied confidently to all of my queries however, and for all intent and purpose logically seemed to be a good fit for the company.

From his initial greeting and handshake however two little words kept bouncing around in my head like a ping pong ball and as much as I tried to dismiss them, the words 'sticky fingers' played again and again.

I had no basis for these two words, they were just there. Rationally his paperwork seemed in order and nothing he said or did led me to doubt or question him. Yet there they were those two little words. I made a mental note of them.

Some would interpret those words literally and wonder if perhaps there was an aroma of the Cinnamon Danish he might have had for breakfast or his nervousness had made his hands and fingers sticky for some reason. In relation to this particular situation at hand, it meant things would stick to those fingers and those 'things' would be company property. To me, it meant theft.

After he departed I began the next leg of my process which was checking his references. In every case I received acceptable feedback on his performance yet not one organization stated that they would hire him back. Oddly each company gave the same reason; it was against their policy to rehire.

I approached my employer with my unsubstantiated concerns. I was told this young man was the son of my employers' best friend therefore we would be hiring him even if he had two heads and eight legs, regardless of any worries I may have. I then asked if he could at least be placed in an area of the company where, if my fears were legitimate, he could do the least damage. I was informed he would be placed in the Distribution Centre on the night shift. Talk about letting the wolf into the hen house.

I was so vehement in my opinion that I had my employer sign a release recognizing how opposed I was to this particular hire. It's called covering your behind. The release was placed in this young man's HR file.

The young man seemed to fit in well enough although there were some who just couldn't seem to warm to him. He offered to stay late, come in on weekends and if the supervisor was stuck, particularly on a Friday night, he would certainly close for him. Two months went by without incident but somehow inventory seemed slightly off through month three, then month four. By month five, serious questions were being raised about the Distribution Centre and inventory discrepancies.

I again broached the question of this young man but as before my concerns fell on deaf ears. After all he was the best friends' son. What more needed to be said.

As these inventory discrepancies escalated police were finally notified and security surveillance installed. Just on a gut feeling I suggested they focus on loading dock 8 at the end of the warehouse and watch for activity Friday evenings around 11:30, in particular to watch for a white cube van. The police wanted to know how I knew this and what my connection was. I explained it was just a feeling. The officer I was speaking with simply smirked and shook his head as he jotted down my thoughts.

Two weeks later, on a Friday night around 11:30 p.m. surveillance cameras caught a white cube van backing up to loading dock 8. There, front and centre, helping two others load thousands of dollars of product into the van, was the best friend's son.

Unfortunately because of the relationship my employer had with this young man's father, charges were never laid, the young man was discreetly laid off and the issue was closed.

Immediately following this young man's quiet dismissal, my employer called me into his office and pointed an accusing finger at me. He ranted that I was responsible for hiring this young man therefore I was negligent in protecting the company and in his opinion that was grounds for termination and I too should be fired.

Shocked by his verbal attack I excused myself momentarily and returned with that wonderful little release he had scoffed at signing only months before. He glanced at it briefly, reddened slightly before tossing it back at me and quietly advised me to 'make sure it never happened again.'

To satisfy my curiosity I backtracked on each and every prior employer this young man had. It is illegal to give a negative reference however sometimes less said means more. I reconnected with each reference and asked only two questions; was the young man hired because of a friend or family connection and would the term 'sticky fingers' seem to have some relevance where this young mans' employment was concerned.

In every case this nice well dressed and well mannered young man had acquired his jobs through daddy's contacts. In every case it seemed he had stolen in some form and in every case no charges were ever laid. As with our situation, friendships run deep therefore in each prior instance he was just quietly let go. I doubt his father ever knew the real reason behind his son's repeated terminations.

As for me, had I not heeded those two little semi-subliminal words bouncing around in my head I too would have been terminated. Sticky fingers turned out to be my saving grace.

IN THE BEGINNING

From an early age I have had an uncanny ability to read people. At the tender age of twenty-one, I was asked to take on the role of Personnel Manager for a large organization embarking on a massive and rapid expansion. During this time I was also asked by other organizations to give my input, on contract basis, where key employees were being interviewed for hire.

One particular multi-million dollar company contracted me for several months to screen resumes and take potential applicants through the initial interview stages. Once short-listed the company policy was to send the resumes to a firm that specialized in reference and background checks. When the reference checks returned I would then take those qualified and arrange interviews with the Executives. They were doing a very rapid mass hire to accommodate new business and there were a number of key executive positions to be filled. Obviously only those short-listed would be reference checked but just by sheer volume of positions to be filled I was submitting between forty and sixty qualified applications per week to be screened.

As with any organization, people are amazing assets to a firm when the right people are placed in the right positions. However personnel can also be a huge financial liability if mistakes are made when hiring, even the initial hiring stages can be costly.

About a month into my tenure I received a call from my contact at the firm that checked references. He knew I was on contract and not a regular employee so he asked me about my background and how I seemed to select such stellar applicants. He stated that most who submit for references average about forty to fifty percent success rate, sixty percent would be extremely high. My submissions however were coming back ninety-eight percent successful. He wanted to know what process I used to select my candidates.

He was stunned when I explained to him that I trusted my first sensory impressions by perceiving traits from their name and application before reviewing the resume and applicant as one normally would. I then blended the two sets of information to make my final evaluation. He was dumbfounded. I expressed to him that it was an actual process and as long as I trusted my process I got the results I needed. It was also the reason I was brought in as I could reduce the hiring time by two-thirds in some cases, again saving time and money for the company in the long run.

The Executives also began to notice the calibre of the applicants being put through and asked if I would attend the Executive interviews as well and give my feedback. From that step it went to a simple 'yes hire immediately with no Executive interview necessary' if that application had my initials on it. In a matter of weeks I had gained the full trust of Management and Executives to place the right people in the right positions based not only on qualifications but just as importantly on personality trait matching.

One Senior Vice President did question a particular hiring. He was extremely upset with this specific new hire as she didn't seem to have the required skills or experience he had asked for. Looking at the individual's paperwork I didn't recognize the name as someone I had interviewed or reference checked. Moreover my initials and notes were nowhere to be found. I asked where this new employee came from and soon discovered that the Human Resources Manager had presented this candidate for hire on her own (nepotism is a wonderful thing in the working world), which of course was her right in her position, however this VP simply assumed this new hire had come through me.

The Senior VP was furious. "I thought she was one of yours so I just automatically gave the go-ahead to hire her, I didn't even interview her" he stated emphatically. "What am I supposed to do with her now, she's useless." I pointed out that my initials and comments were not on the paperwork so all I could do was suggest he speak with his HR Manager and if possible either reposition her in a more suitable job within the company or exercise the company's three-month probationary clause to dismiss her. I also encouraged him to act sooner than later as once an employee is past their probationary period they are yours and there are legal ramifications for dismissal. We joked about the situation later – once he found a suitable replacement.

Over the years I have had CEO's, Company Presidents and Executives ask me to circle a room and introduce myself to attendees prior to a critical meeting and then discreetly give my initial impressions of how to position the presentation or the meeting, who the key players at the meeting really were and what the outcome of the meeting would be.

Most who have attained these Senior and Executive stations of success already have finely honed interpersonal skills and not necessarily in need of additional input but often too these individuals are used to running so much on left-brain logic, sometimes those initial hunches and gut feelings slide by unnoticed. It is often those initial impressions that can lead to success or not. My input was always requested and then applied if, when, and where it was beneficial. Like having an ace in your pocket to use if you choose to.

I am not unique, I simply use that innate ability we all have to perceive, but are conditioned not to. When we do exercise our first impressions we often then rationalize them away and proceed with what seems most logical. To be truly effective, both initial awareness and logical deductions need to be acknowledged and be exercised in unison with each other.

OPEN YOUR EYES, EARS, MIND, HEART

STEP BOLDLY PAST YOUR FEARS

It is human nature to shy away from the unknown and in many cases be fearful of it. Before we begin I would like to share the following story with you.

A very dear elderly friend of mine once told me about one of her very first jobs many years ago. She was recruited to go door to door selling a very innovative service that was new to the area and soon to be installed in the neighbourhood - did these homeowners want access to this particular service?

She said she has never had so many doors slammed in her face! In some instances the door was simply slammed shut on her while in other cases she received an 'ear full' prior to the slamming of the door. She heard comments such as 'this is witchcraft', 'what you are offering is evil and the work of the devil', and 'no good will come of this, mark my words'.

She never took the rejections personally, just noted how sadly narrow-minded some individuals were as she would proceed to the next house.

What was she offering that was causing such anger, resentment and fear? Electricity. Electrical wiring to be installed on the street and then run from the street into each individual home – did the homeowner want to hook up or not?

People are funny when faced with the unknown and instead of exploring and embracing what is new and different, it is human nature to resist it. Sometimes when we open that door of resistance even just a crack, we open ourselves up to a whole new world of awareness that we can harness and benefit from.

WHAT IS TRAIT READING?

Trait Reading is a method of gaining insight, information and otherwise unattainable knowledge about the traits of a person, organization, stock name, place, event or situation.

Whether we consciously recognize it or not our subconscious is continually processing sensory perceptions and relaying them to our brains. Rather than ignoring or dismissing them, we can use these semi-subliminal perceptions to our advantage in all we do. Trait Reading is the process of training the brain to consciously recognize those subconscious impressions; just as you train your brain to recognize and calculate a mathematical question; understand a new language; or follow recipe instructions. With practice applying Trait Reading techniques, you will be able to accurately and instinctually evaluate an individual's main personality traits and characteristics or the traits of a situation within 10 seconds.

Interpreting body language is now a recognized and well used practice corporately and privately. The understanding and application of Trait Reading is yet another level of awareness that goes beyond body language in the fascinating realm of communication.

The actual method of Trait Reading involves acquiring and blending information from three Levels of awareness then adding this to the knowledge you now gain with your current techniques and methods.

The first Level of Trait Reading information is pure subliminal and semi-subliminal sensory awareness (hereinafter referred to as Sensory Awareness). It is our immediate reaction, thoughts, sensory impressions, hunches or gut feelings we get about someone or something. The connection that triggers this sensory awareness can be as simple as a phone conversation, seeing someone from a distance or coming in contact with a picture, voice, name, object or possession.

That first fleeting impression and awareness is what determines if we comfortably continue walking toward someone or cross the street because we feel anxious about who is approaching. It is this instant sensation of ease or anxiety that comes from the very instinctual core of our being. It is these impressions that we are taught to dismiss or second guess from a very early age. By the time we reach adulthood we have tuned them out to such a degree we barely acknowledge them, if at all. It is this first Level of awareness that is the most significant and accurate yet least regarded.

The second Level of acquiring Trait Reading insight and information is through Name Analysis. What does the sight and sound of your Name actually reveal to others about you and to you about them? How is this knowledge beneficial to you?

The very sound of a name emits a vibration that resonates with you or it does not. The appearance of that name will also appeal to your senses or not. Both the auditory sound and the visual appearance of a name will create an immediate sensory impression and reaction. Again, it is these sensory impressions we are also often oblivious to or absently dismiss.

The composition of a name reveals the traits of the living entity it is connected to: A person's name alone will reveal much about that individual's energy and personality traits: A company name will reflect the combined energy and traits of the owners and employees of that company: A stock name will reflect the energy and combined traits of the investors in that company: A place with reflect the energy of the inhabitants, and so on.

By analyzing and interpreting what the letters, letter placement, sight and sound of a name means Name Analysis uses a practical format to define a person's most basic personality traits or the fundamentals of a place or situation. We can then build and apply a trait profile to issues, situations, communication and decisions at hand. A Name also acts as the sensory 'anchor' or 'connector' providing additional Sensory Awareness to our logical Name Analysis information.

The third Level of Trait Reading is by recognizing an individual's Brain Wiring through their very words and actions - what they actually say and do. Why does someone think and act that way, how does that impact you and vice versa? This is not body language, it goes beyond that. A person's most basic words and actions reveal if they are left, right or whole brain oriented; if they are builders or maintainers; do they see issues as black and white or shades of grey. Are they nurturers and caregivers, or teachers and educators? Each area gives you fundamental knowledge to understand and connect with another better or perhaps differently than you may have without this added awareness.

The final step is taking these three Levels of information and effectively combining them with your current methods of reasoning about a person, organization, investment or situation at hand: This is Trait Reading.

As indicated with 'sticky fingers', Trait Reading fits incredibly well with hiring processes and personality matching when blended with traditional means of evaluating skillsets and experience. Other ways I have professionally used my ability to Trait Read over the years includes large organization insolvency and bankruptcy cases, insurance embezzlement cases, fraud, theft, jury selection, legal issues and criminal investigations.

Where my clients' personal lives have been concerned, Trait Reading has been invaluable giving additional insight with relationship analysis, family conflicts, mental/emotional issues, divorces, custody issues, abuse situations and personal injury suits. I have worked extensively with parents struggling with their teens, and teens who needed guidance and self-awareness about their natural talents and appropriate career choices.

Trait Reading is the overall technique I have applied over the last twenty plus years in my personal and business decision-making as the means of attaining non-traditional insightful information about people and situations. Trait Reading gives invaluable awareness and understanding and a deeper clarity to all areas of your life than you have ever possessed. It is instinctual. You will begin to draw on it naturally once you understand it fully.

Imagine how you will benefit from a method that gives you otherwise unattainable information about a spouse, partner, child, parent, co-worker, employer, business associate, customer or situation in your life. Think of how pertinent this knowledge will be when assessed, analyzed and combined with your present logical deductions and decisions.

We as humans often complicate things to a point where we get lost in the process when often it is attention to and using the most basic components that gives us the greatest awareness and results. I have always believed in the 'KIS' principle (keep it simple), as it eliminates the added processes that often end up confusing us rather than clarifying.

The technique of Trait Reading puts a workable structure and method to perceiving. Trait Reading takes us back to understanding and applying those very basic elements of recognition and awareness we should all be using and benefiting from in all we do.

Part 1

LEVEL 1

SENSORY AWARENESS

(Hunches, Thoughts, Gut Feelings, Sensory Impressions)

If it is human nature and part of our actual brain functionality to get hunches, gut feelings, sensory thoughts and ideas about people and situations why are we so quick to dismiss them? If indeed we could recognize these impressions and harness our power and ability to use them, could we then integrate them effectively into our personal and business-related choices and decisions?

Scientific research has proven as shown through photography, scanning techniques, etc. that all living things possess energy fields around them and emit a distinct vibration from this energy field.

We ourselves subconsciously evaluate an individual's vibration and energy field prior to consciously assessing their physical body. Hence, that instant sense of being attracted to or repelled by someone, yet we can't rationalize why.

INTUITIVE SENSORY IMPRESSIONS - WHAT *DO* WE EMIT & RECEIVE?

Trait Reading uses the portion of our brain that subliminally and semi-subliminally recognizes and interprets the energy field and vibration everyone emits, then takes this semi-subliminal information and uploads it to conscious awareness just as a computer would upload data to be processed.

This initial sensory impressions or feelings about a situation or a person come simultaneously in two forms; feelings and emotions, and thoughts and ideas. The sensory indicators you may receive as feelings or emotions can be uneasiness versus calmness, brightness versus darkness, optimism or oppression, sometimes even a feeling of hot or cold, or a fleeting feeling of happiness, sadness, joy, anger or frustration. If our Sensory Awareness to something or someone is particularly negative it can also come in the form of an actual physical reaction such as a sinking feeling in the pit of the stomach, a brief wave of nausea, a feeling of tensing up, or breaking into a light sweat.

For example if you noted the name of a particular stock you wanted to invest in and had a fleeting sense of foreboding, darkness or cold, all of which have negative connotations for most, your trait reading would be negative. You would then apply that instant reaction and sensory impression to your question of should you invest? Your Sensory Awareness is immediately telling you the investment will have a negative outcome.

On the conscious level of thoughts and ideas, you may actually hear words in your mind such as my 'sticky fingers' or even see the words 'yes' or 'no' in your mind. You may have a related idea pop into your head which you recognize as either positive or negative. It may also come in the form of a memory triggered by the person or situation at hand. Again using the name of a stock as an example, you may ask about the feasibility of one particular stock yet have totally different stock come to mind. In this case you would acknowledge the dynamics of that different stock; is it a success or a disaster, slow growth, decline, or like a shooting star? You would then use those impressions as indicators and the benchmark for the original stock you are inquiring about.

If you have an ability to visualize you may see in your mind an actual graph or chart depicting the direction of the stock. Your conscious impressions will be very crisp, concise and feel logical but they will come so quickly as that instant thought you won't have time to *think* about it. Your information in the form of feelings and emotions will often come in unison with your thoughts and ideas. Take all of it and note it. These Sensory Awareness initial impressions are fleeting so make sure you acknowledge them sufficiently enough to retain the essence of the impressions. Do not dismiss any impressions and do not analyze them at this point. Document them wherever possible. This is the Trait Reader information you will ultimately couple with your logically-based thoughts, ideas and means you presently use in your decision making.

So where do we become conflicted? When someone assures us the investment is viable or the facts around the investment support a success track. What we then do is rationalize based on logic and dismiss those initial impressionistic thoughts, feelings and ideas. If the outcome is indeed negative, we regret not listening to ourselves in the first place – as we knew we should have.

The other negative component with decision-making is our need to assure ourselves with advice from all of our nearest and dearest. Our social conditioning of that need to be perfect and never make a mistake or be wrong, leads us to trust those around us more than we trust ourselves. Again second guessing the very Reading information we generate and we should rely on first and foremost.

Several years ago a popular radio announcer and client of mine was asked to help raise money for charity by going onstage and choosing Door #1, Door #2, or Door #3. Behind one of those doors was a $10,000 donation. Her instant initial thought was Door #3. The M/C asked if that was her final decision while the audience shouted out which door they felt was best. She hesitated momentarily, second-guessed herself, listened to the audience and changed her decision to Door #1. To her dismay she discovered the $10,000 was behind her original selection, Door #3. She was furious with herself for changing from her sensory awareness and initial thought.

Conditioning and fear of what is unknown is our worst enemy and what usually holds us back. From the earliest age we are taught what to do and not do. We gauge all we do by how perfectly we complete a task. This can be as simple as a three year old trying their best to colour within the lines to writing an exam at school. Every aspect of our lives from personal to academic to our work environment as adults is measured by others in increments of perfectionism and success.

We have lost the ability to evaluate our lives based by an experiential measuring stick. We have also lost the ability to use all of our senses effectively as we are so bombarded and overloaded with sensory input. We have lost the power to actually quiet our minds enough to hear ourselves and heed our own guidance and direction. Trait Reading will help you regain this lost natural talent.

WHAT IF WE 'DETECT' SOMETHING NEGATIVE?

Simple. Take it and use it to your advantage. Yet again though as soon as we even start to perceive a negative of some form we revert to our fears, shut down and block it. Life is a series of positives and negatives all woven together to produce the final result of our lives as a whole. If we detect something negative for ourselves, freedom of choice allows us to make changes which may alter the outcome. If the negative impressions involve someone else we can relay the information we are receiving. It is then up to them to use this information as they wish. They then have freedom of their choices and decisions to use the information to their advantage or not. This is where we become so bottlenecked by ourselves. Life is not always meant to be a perfect bed of roses. It is meant to have its trials and tribulations, ups and downs, positives and negatives. Sometimes it is actually the negatives and struggles that become our greatest successes and learning.

I have always believed that the words 'right' and 'wrong' should be removed from our vocabulary as every single thing we experience in our lives brings a positive awareness and outcome of some form. We may not see this initially if the issues at hand seem heart-breaking or insurmountable, but it is that old saying 'this too shall pass' that allows us to take that deep breath and carry on. Often times it is also what we instantly perceive as our greatest mistake (another word we should remove) which reaps our greatest reward.

When we remove the fear and apprehension we actually begin to view life differently and remove our limitations. Rather than resisting or supressing we begin to view our lives and experiences as opportunities, growth and awareness.

As soon as this happens our ability to Trait Read expands incredibly as we no longer consciously and subconsciously try to filter and guard against everything unusual we are sensing, feeling and thinking. We open ourselves up to experiences without self-imposed boundaries.

ENGAGE ALL OF YOUR SENSES:

As mentioned previously we have to a great degree unintentionally shut our senses down. When we revert back to acknowledging how we are perceiving our information we will realize that in addition to hearing, sensing and feeling as we have addressed, it can also come in the form of smell, taste, and simply knowing – but not knowing how you know – you just know.

For example if you connect with someone new and your very first sense is a fleeting awareness of freshly baked bread which reminds you of your mother who you adored, then the connection with that new person should be read as positive for you. If however, your first thought upon meeting someone new leaves a brief sour taste in your mouth, you can bet that is how your relationship with that individual will be, sour.

I had a man share his car buying experience with me. He went into a dealership to purchase a new car and found three models he was partial to yet the third vehicle he felt hesitant and unsettled about. As he discussed his choices and options, the salesman insisted he could give him a better price on that third vehicle. It would be a great deal. The particulars on this third vehicle seemed comparable to the other two yet every time this man looked at the paperwork for this third vehicle the thought of a lemon popped to mind. The impression was so strong he said he could almost taste the sourness of the lemon. As he couldn't rationalize this bizarre thought and feeling (no the car was not lemon yellow it was actually deep blue) he took the deal and bought 'the lemon'.

Not surprising, the problems actually started on the way home from the dealership. Within five blocks the brand new car simply died at a traffic light. As everything was under warranty the dealership agreed to honour all warranties but refused to take the vehicle back. However after four months of constant problems and attempted repairs the manufacturer themselves labelled the car a 'lemon' and replaced it with the same make and model. The new car never caused a single problem. As for the owner, he cursed himself every day during those four months for not listening to and trusting himself. He does chuckle about it now though when he recounts the story.

Every one of our senses comes into play with Sensory Awareness. Our sense of smell, sight, sound, taste and touch are all contributing factors in providing usable information. We may see something visually which creates an impression. We may picture something in our mind that gives us insight. When we touch or hold an object we will have an instant sensory reaction of some kind. Our sense of smell is one of our strongest impressionistic senses and will often trigger memories which will be associative to our situation or question at hand. Sounds also are memory evoking and what may be a comfortable sound or tone to one may be disturbing to another. And just as the man purchasing the car stated he could almost taste the sourness of 'the lemon', our sense of taste is significant in Sensory Awareness. We just need to pay attention to it.

'To each his own' as the saying goes applies to Sensory Awareness and impressions. One of the things I point out in my classes is individualism and uniqueness in perceiving as no two individuals will ever perceive the same thing in the same way. As perceptions are unique to the individual, their background and their experiences, there can never be right or wrong perceptions only what is correct for that individual. Therefore if I asked five participants for their Sensory Awareness to the same question I would expect five different answers. All responses would be varied yet valid based on their unique sensory impressions and interpretation.

SUBLIMINAL EXCHANGE:

We constantly subliminally exchange information by what our vibration and energy field emits to others and what we perceive from theirs. When I interviewed that thieving young man years ago, his intent to steal was so strongly ingrained in his character that it literally jumped out at me. It was also the reason many in the company never felt comfortable with him but couldn't justify why. Although his words and actions portrayed him as considerate, caring and a team player, his energy and vibration emitted his true traits and intent. It was the extreme contradiction between his negative energy and his falsely positive words and actions that others were subliminally confused by and therefore leery of.

When you meet someone for the first time do you instantly experience a feeling of liking or disliking them? Do you feel comfortable with them or unsettled? Trusting or distrusting? Have you ever felt as if you've known someone forever yet you just met them? Or on the contrary, you couldn't warm to them if your life depended on it but you don't know why?

If your initial reaction feels negative it does not necessarily indicate that someone is 'bad'. It means your energies and vibration are incongruent with theirs in some way. If there actually is a negative component to that individual however, your senses will be heightened, recognize it and alert you accordingly. All you need to do is listen to yourself.

How often have you said or heard someone else say 'I've never met a (person's name) I liked or got along with. It isn't as much the name you dislike you actually don't resonate with the energy traits associated with it. Because it is our nature to rationalize everything, we tie this dislike to something tangible, which is often their name.

We have no logical basis for these immediate thoughts and feelings which are fleeting but definite. These are our semi-subliminal impressions of their 'tuning fork' vibration, energy field and traits.

ENERGY FIELD WIDTH & INTERACTION:

Every person, their energy field and vibration emits both positive and negative components and fluctuates in relation to what is going on around them. Everything has the balance of yin and yang, a combination of both to produce the whole. Energy fields and vibrational rates are indicative of culture only in relation to the width of their energy field. Those from less densely populated areas generally have wider energy fields giving others the impression that they are more open, receptive and easy to establish rapport with. Those from highly overpopulated countries tend to have a closer, narrower energy field around their physical body. If the environment is constantly overcrowded an individual will subconsciously hold their energy field closer in an attempt to minimize others unintentionally violating their personal space. The narrower the energy field, the more secretive, private and guarded they will seem to others.

When we are happy or in a positive frame of mind our energy field expands and our vibration rises. As we subliminally seem more open, others will automatically be drawn to us. When we are feeling sad, hurt, or negative we draw our energy field closer to us to buffer and protect ourselves from whatever is causing the negative in our lives. It is what others often refer to as 'one reverting into themselves' or 'closing themselves off'. Others will subconsciously steer clear, sensing that for some reason that individual 'needs their own space'. Isn't it funny how without even realizing it we coin phrases that define what is going on energetically?

Think of examples of energy being 'thrown' around in your workplace and home environment. We have all known individuals who purposely enter another's space to create either an assertive or intimidating environment, making the individual on the receiving end uncomfortable, easier to manipulate and control. How do employees react when an Executive enters the workspace? There is an involuntary instinctive tensing. Why? Whether intentional or not, an Executive emits a significantly different vibration, which is felt instantly.

Regardless of the relationship, an employee will subconsciously alter their behaviour automatically to adjust to the new vibration being emitted by their senior. This interaction is an example of the 'ripple effect', which occurs continuously as we move in and out of each other's energy fields.

It is also this energy field and vibration we are drawn to with politicians, celebrities, rock stars, elite athletes, religious figures, those in positions of power and success. We often refer to it as their charisma or their magnetic personality. We may not know them personally but we are enamoured with them nonetheless.

EXPLORING THE POWER OF OUR ENERGY & VIBRATION:

Some may feel that Trait Reading into another is an invasion of privacy yet how often in the past has someone misinterpreted what you have said or done. Likewise perhaps you have misread them and felt that neither of you are communicating effectively. Gaining insight into another person's thoughts and feelings or a situation can be pure value-add in enhancing relationships, producing better business results, achieving mutual goals faster and easier, and making life in general more harmonious for yourself and those around you. Trait Reading also gives us a way to look inward at ourselves as individuals, how we perceive and interact with everything around us.

Whether we like it or not our energy fields and vibrations continuously flow in and out of one another's. This natural process subconsciously relays our innermost thoughts and feelings to those around us. Although others may not consciously recognize the precise content of what is going on in our heads and our hearts, they will perceive even our most subtle vibrational changes. They will question what is different and wonder why. This is often when we question 'was it something I did or something I said?' Frequently though we discover it isn't about us at all and relates to something entirely different. This subconscious exchange is also what triggers such comments as 'I was just thinking the same thing', or 'too funny, you must have read my mind'. It also extends to instinctively finishing each other's sentences because you just knew what the other person was going to say.

This energy and vibration extends further than physical presence. How often have you thought of someone and they call a short time later or you reach for that ringing phone already knowing who is calling you. Usually we chuckle at 'the coincidence'.

Just as electronic transmissions from television, radio, emails, texts, etc. shoot across our atmospheric airwaves, we too have the power to project to others along our own energetic airwaves. Even across thousands of miles we can project our thoughts and feelings to others, particularly when these emotions are highly charged.

Wartime is when our emotional energies are heightened to the extreme.

During the Second World War my mother's cousin who was five at this particular point in time was outside playing late one morning when he heard his father's voice very clearly call his name three times. Excited that his father was finally home from overseas, this little boy raced into the house to greet him.

The little boy's mother was in the kitchen having coffee with a friend. She asked her son what all the excitement was about. "Daddy's home, Daddy's home, I heard him call my name, he called me three times, where is he Mommy"?

Although this was not possible but to appease her son she searched through the house and checked outside. There was no trace of her husband who, as she knew, was still with his battalion in Europe.

Returning to the kitchen she glanced at the clock on the wall, which read 11:00 a.m. and as she always did while her husband was away, mentally calculated what time it would be for him overseas.

Her son was inconsolable. "I'm not lying, I heard him, Mommy. He called my name three times." The little boy sobbed in her arms until he cried himself to sleep.

Shortly thereafter she received a telegram stating that her husband had been killed in battle the very day her son had heard his father calling to him.

After the War a fellow soldier came to visit. He wanted her to know he not only fought with her husband and was at his side on the battlefield the day her husband died, they had become steadfast friends.

He explained how he had cradled her husband and his dear friend during his final moments and how it had broken this soldier's heart to hear her husband cry out his son's name three times before he took his last breath.

Shaking as this soldier recounted the events of her husband's passing she asked if he recalled approximately what time her husband died. "...I remember looking at my watch...it was 17:00 hours so I guess that would have been...11:00 a.m. your time."

"Thank you," she replied quietly.

This little boy, from thousands of miles away, heard his father's final words. Energetically his father had come home one last time to reconnect with his son.

This is the incredible power of connection with those around us we possess. Now knowing the instinctual abilities you have to perceive another from five inches, to five yards, to five thousand miles away, how do you tap into it and become more attuned? In simplest form, start paying attention to the sensations you experience from those around you. Make mental note of similarities, differences, feelings of comfort and unsettle. Then ask yourself why. Make it a game for yourself, with no grades or rights or wrongs, just experiences and heightened awareness. By merely paying more attention to the energies around you in relation to your own, you will begin to significantly enhance your perceptive abilities.

TO START BUILDING YOUR TRAIT READING PROFILE:

Always begin with your immediate Sensory Awareness and impressions, being sure to note even the most subtle thoughts and feelings. Where there are concerns with your information (such as 'sticky fingers'), analyze your impressions further or make inquiries if possible to validate the facts or basis to your

Trait profile. Always trust your initial semi-subliminally-based perceptions first and foremost above and beyond all else.

If your perceptions don't make sense to you acknowledge them anyway and then put interpretation to them as they relate to you and the situation or person in question, just as we discussed earlier. Remember you are gaining insight into another and what doesn't make sense or apply to you may be relevant to the individual or situation you are inquiring about.

Keep in mind too as we have discussed that just as we are all individuals, we all perceive differently. What may be viewed as a positive to one may be negative for another. Sensory Awareness applies uniquely to you and your perceptions and therefore open to your interpretation.

For example, one woman I worked with wanted insight into the man she had recently started dating. She was unsure of him but couldn't understand why. When I asked her what her immediate impression was when she thought of him she laughingly replied that all she had come to mind was an egg. Just one egg. She was puzzled. I asked her how she felt about eggs. She replied that she ate them once in a while but as a regular diet they made her quite nauseous. She could go months without them. She liked her eggs over-easy not hard boiled and stated that eggs are fragile and need to be handled gently so as not to crack or break them.

I then asked her to take those thoughts and apply them to her question about this man in her life. She thought momentarily and deduced that she enjoyed his company once in a while but found him persistent and somewhat controlling therefore not someone she wanted as a steady diet in her life, just the thought of it made her queasy. He wasn't as easy going (over easy) as she liked and at times he was very hard-headed (hard boiled). She also commented that he was very set in his ways, seemed to be a bit of a loner and usually put his wants first ahead of hers; hence her impression of just one egg.

She went on to state that he seemed like a very nice man but often during their conversations he seemed quite scattered as if his thoughts were scrambled and he could be quite opinionated which she found frustrating. She chuckled at the pun as she remarked how she often felt she was 'walking on egg shells' around him as he could be moody and difficult to communicate with sometimes.

She summed up her thoughts by stating that perhaps this particular 'egg-head' wasn't for her.

Her perceptions and resulting conclusions were negative, however if I were to ask someone else what an egg meant to them and they loved eggs in any form and could happily make a steady diet of them their interpretation would be positive in relation to their question or situation.

Begin your Trait Reading Profile with what is familiar to you. Even if you already know the individual or circumstances, still tap into your senses and Sensory Awareness and begin to build the profile. Just by going through the exercise you will begin to understand the dynamics and traits of the person or situation to a greater degree.

SENSORY AWARENESS &
IMPRESSIONS - PROFILE

(As soon as you write down the name or situation in question note your immediate initial sensory awareness, thoughts, feelings, ideas and impressions that come to mind and emotion. Once you start actually *thinking* of what you should write, you are no longer accessing Sensory Awareness so stop writing. You may receive a little or a lot, some may make sense and some may not but all of it will be relevant so document everything you perceive. As you read through the remaining sections additional sensory information will continually come to mind. There is a Sensory Awareness page at the end of every section for your notations but document your impressions as you go along as they will come to you randomly while reading through each section.)

INDIVIDUAL OR SITUATION IN QUESTION:

_____

_____

SENSORY AWARENESS & IMPRESSIONS:

THOUGHTS:

_____
_____
_____
_____
_____
_____
_____

FEELINGS:

_____

_____

_____

_____

_____

_____

_____

Part 2

LEVEL 2

NAME ANALYSIS TRAITS

(A Blend of Core Traits and Life Traits)

As every animate living thing emits a particular energy, inanimate objects around us absorb this energy that we emit. Whether animate or inanimate, everything has a name of some form. It is this connection between a Name and associated energy field/vibration that is the second Level of awareness we can tap into to gain additional knowledge and information.

WHAT THE VIBRATION & ENERGY FIELD OF OUR VERY NAME REVEALS

(Information We Subliminally Impress Upon Others)

Years ago a very prominent woman in our community named Barbara had an afternoon tea for all other 'Barbara's' who would like to attend. Over the years she had met a number of women with the same name as hers and they all seemed to have very similar personality traits. This peaked her interest so to quell her curiosity she had this tea.

To her surprise and pleasure she had a good turnout. As she mingled with her guests she discovered a significant number of similarities between all of them. Most had the same likes, dislikes, tastes in decorating, in furniture and colours; most had strong-willed personalities and were goal oriented and most had experienced childhood instability of some form even though they were from all different walks of life.

There was no other reason for the tea other than an opportunity for like-named and oddly enough like-minded women to come together. The only common denominator between all of them was the same first name.

HOW A NAME CONNECTS YOU:

Using a Name simply acts as an 'anchor' or 'aid' to create another impressionistic connection and means of awareness. The letter configuration of the name itself creates a certain energy field and emits a particular vibrational rate from the individual, which can be quickly and precisely interpreted, whether read, heard, in person, or at a distance.

Trait Reading through Name Analysis also applies to names of inanimate objects such as names of stocks, investments, companies, locations, buildings, and events as all of these 'things' have absorbed and then emit the combined human energies connected to them (the employees of a company; the investors in a stock; the residents of a town; the creator of a building; the organizers and participants of an event.) Everyone and everything has a name and energy of some form that can be interpreted and read. Name Analysis information is broken into two components; Core Traits and Life Traits. Both create the overall essence and interpretation of the Name Analysis and Name Traits.

24

This raises the question about changing your name completely or changing the spelling. It is a 'which came first the horse or the cart' scenario and both can apply depending on circumstances. Does your personality, vibration and energy field change because of a situation in your life, which then urges you to change your name to one more reflective of your new energy and vibration? Or do you change your name to help change your personality, vibration and energy to match the energy of the newly acquired name? Do you maintain the name of a floundering company or do you alter it to a stronger name hoping to create a different more successful energy around the firm? Or do you change the individuals running the struggling organization to alter the unsuccessful path it is currently on by infusing a different type of energy through new staff?

Either way, when you intentionally change a name it is because something in you or connected to you has changed. If you change your name radically it means you either want to disassociate from some aspect of your life or something in your life has forced your personality to shift. The new name would reflect this radical shift. When you learn the components of Name Analysis however you will understand that even what seems to be a radical name change, (unless someone is aware of name vibration and energy association), may unintentionally select a name with the same Core Traits and characteristics as their previous name.

To give a simple example, I went on vacation with a very dear friend and a fairly large number of people connected to her. Although I had socialized with one particular woman in this group previously, she jokingly stated that she simply couldn't remember my name therefore she was going to call me Darryl. Hence for the remainder of the vacation I became known as Darryl.

However, if you analyze the two names Deborah and Darryl as we will do shortly, the energy and vibration is comparable. She may have changed the name however unknowingly she assigned a name that contained the same base personality traits and characteristics that truly reflected the essence of me.

Remember too, even as you exam the dynamics of a name, have a conversation or review someone's documentation, your subtle almost subliminal semi-subliminal initial awareness and impressions will continue and should be noted and treated as your first line of relevant information.

The traits and characteristics revealed by the very letters and positioning of the name becomes your second avenue of more factual information. Then this impressionistic technique is added to our logical thought processes and decisions about people and situations in our lives. It is not meant to replace your present analytical rationale. It is the blending of these two trains of thought and awareness that give us a more profound final result.

CORE TRAITS OF A NAME:

An individual's Core personality traits are reflected in the name given at birth. Even though parents think they are consciously choosing their baby's name, they are actually being guided subconsciously to select a name that will most closely reflect the baby's Soul and personality traits. How often have we heard of parents changing a baby's name from their original choice once the baby arrives because the name did not seem to fit. Their initial choice was incongruent with their baby's energy field and vibrational rate.

And what of parent's naming their child after another family member? It isn't as much of a struggle if that family member has passed. It is not an issue if the name is given as the middle name, but for a child to be given the same first name as a living relative can cause huge conflict for the child.

Every child needs to have their own name as they have their own personality, vibration and energy field. These children who carry a living members' first name will often alter or change their given name completely or use their middle name to disassociate from the namesake family member. This has nothing to do with lack of love or respect for that family member. It has to do with basic traits, individuality and Soul recognition.

Many new names are appearing and many names being chosen sound stronger and more determined to accommodate our rapidly changing competitive environment. Parents want to give their child a sense of uniqueness enabling them to 'stand out in the crowd'. A unique name is one way of achieving this. Without realizing it, parents are subconsciously trying to give their child an edge with that unique name so they won't be lost in the masses. Sometimes to make their child unique by changing the spelling of their name for example, the name is so convoluted that others struggle to pronounce it. This is when parents consciously modify their initial selection, which creates a totally different energy and vibration to what that baby inherently has. Hence the energy of the name will no longer fit the energy of the child. If the name is difficult to spell or pronounce it can lead to embarrassment, discomfort, resentment and frustration for the child if they constantly have to correct others.

When working with Name Analysis surnames or last names are irrelevant. You only want to use the name the person presently uses as well as their full first name given at birth if that name differs in some way. It is also essential to know if they use their second name rather than their first given name.

As stated, at birth each person is physically unique in appearance, mannerisms, habits, voice, perceptions, natural qualities and abilities. These attributes are an individual's Core Traits and it is these Core Traits that define one's initial energy field and vibrational rate.

Now add to this our daily experiences that create conscious shifts in our thoughts, feelings, and actions. These conscious shifts are then reflected in our energy field, our vibration, and what we subconsciously emit to those around us. Minute to minute we are in a state of flux, acting and reacting to all that goes on around us. These experiences, from the simplest to the most profound, create our Life Traits which can shift our outlook, vibration and energy field subtly or significantly. These ongoing shifts and changes add a new dimension and overlay to our basic Core Traits to produce the entire essence of us here and now.

Regardless of shifts and changes in our lives, the basic Core Traits associated with each given name will always remain the same. Therefore we can use the given name as an initial means to identify an individual's fundamental Core personality traits.

Culture, race, colour, nationality and gender are immaterial when discerning the meaning of a name as just like music and a choir, vibration is universal. The exact spelling of a name however is crucial. There is a marked difference between the personalities of 'Mark' and 'Marc' or 'Brian' and 'Bryan' as you will learn.

Think of your life as a choir. It takes the blending of many different voices to create the final unified sound of a choir. Tenors sing together, sopranos sing together, altos sing together and so on. By putting voices with like voices they compliment and support each other. If however you were to mix the different vocals up so a tenor was next to a soprano, who was next to an alto, then asked them to sing, the result would be musical torture to the ears.

All members of the choir may enjoy singing together but when each member is placed with those they most closely harmonize with, sheer musical magic results.

Life is just like the choir. You will always find there are those in your life you 'harmonize' with and those that may 'strike the wrong cord'. Through respect and appreciation of others' individual tones, we can all stand together to produce an amazing 'choir', but choose to surround yourself most closely to those in natural harmony with you.

Now think of yourself individually like a tuning fork within that choir and along with your unique voice you have a unique vibration you radiate to others. Again, you will vibrate in harmony with some and discord with others. One tuning fork pitch and tone is no better or worse than another, just different or similar. Together an amazing overall tone can be created.

Now extend this awareness to the dynamics around the sound of each letter, the names these letters create, the energy and vibration generated by the bearer of that name and what basic Core Trait information can be drawn from them.

HOW DO WE BEGIN...LOGICAL NAME ANALYSIS

CORE TRAITS – INDIVIDUAL LETTERS:

How do we begin to tap into this natural ability of Trait Reading names? What do our names actually disclose about us? Are there some fundamental associative characteristics to letters and names that can give us a quick trait assessment of someone's personality? Let's look at the basics involved with names overall from a logical perspective. Assume individual letters reveal certain traits and when combined into a name the name itself yields additional insight.

What of the letters themselves? The letters of a name are broken into three categories; Strong, Soft and Dual meaning. Strong does not denote power, control or ego and soft does not represent weak, submissive or inferior. Strong letters indicate the individual's overall determination and fortitude while soft expresses the nurturing, caring, compassionate components of one's personality. Just like nature itself there needs to be a blend of strong and soft, yin and yang for overall balance in traits and characteristics. This does not mean names should have equal soft and strong letters. Each individual will have the appropriate combination of strong and soft to reflect the dynamics of who they are and what unique traits they possess. It is these combinations that give us our clues about another.

ADDITIONAL CORE TRAITS OF NAMES:

- When a person shortens their name or uses a shorter nickname it magnifies the strong, stubborn, determined characteristics of the person – their personality has become more 'matter of fact', a 'what you see is what you get' attitude toward life.

- Single syllable names also indicate a person who has a very direct, think what you say and say what you think attitude.

- Changing the spelling of the name indicates a person who is unsettled about their name and identity or needs to distance themselves in some way from the family who named them in order to feel they are being their own person (e.g. James Jr.).

- If you are interpreting a name from paper such as a resume or at a distance, wherever possible acquire the person's age as well for added impressions regarding their Life Traits. If you are interpreting in person age is not necessary since you can visually estimate the individual's approximate age.

- Last names or surnames are irrelevant unless you are looking at the overall generalized traits of an entire family line. For individuals always use the name(s) given at birth along with any modifications they have made during their life.

- A unique name indicates an individual who, like their name, is unique. These individuals tend to be the 'square pegs that don't fit into the round holes' and like to march to their own drummer so to speak. They don't like to lead, will never follow and need to carve their own path regardless of what mainstream society dictates. They are not rebellious rather they just have minds of their own – thank you very much!

STRONG, SOFT & DUAL LETTERS:

STRONG VOWELS:	Y, O, U
STRONG CONSONANTS:	B, D, K, M, N, Q, R
Soft Vowels:	a, e, i
Soft Consonants:	f, h, j, v, w, x, z
Duel Meaning Consonants:	C, G, L, S, P, T

Just like they sound, strong letters (**B, D, K, M, N, O, Q, R, U, Y**) indicate a strong often stubborn personality, confident, determined, focused, results-driven, usually sees issues as black and white, often predominantly left-brain oriented. When we talk about Strong letters they do not refer to power, ego or physical strength. Strong letters indicate a person's trait to handle everything life throws their way, ability to pick themselves up and brush themselves off and conquer all obstacles. When I refer to stubborn as a trait this is not a childish, self-centred stubborn 'I have to have my way' trait, rather the stubbornness I am referring to is that stubbornness to meet all challenges head on, never give up and persevere to find the ways and means around whatever obstacles have been put in your path. That is the definition of stubborn as referred to where trait analysis is concerned.

Soft letters (**a, e, f, h, i, j, v, w, x, z**) indicate a person who is more passively determined, the nurturer, caregiver, wants to make all right with the world, sees the world more in 'grey' rather than black and white, is often more right-brained, usually quite creative.

When looking at the components of a name, the stronger letters will always dominate, however the ratio of strong to soft letters defines the overall personality and placement of the letters also represents particular traits.

When you have soft and strong letters alternating equally throughout the name it indicates balance like the scales of balance or of justice and means the individual always needs to have balance, equality and justice in their lives in order to function 100% effectively. It is also indicative of a person who cannot tolerate racism, bullying or persecution of any kind. If there is imbalance in any area of their lives they will struggle to right all with their world until it is accomplished.

Dual letters *(C, G, L, P, S, T)* can be soft or strong depending on sound, position and the adjacent letters. Dual letters indicate that an individual can choose to be strong, rigid and unbending or gentle, compassionate and accommodating depending on the person or situation they are dealing with. For example the 'P' in Patrick is strong while the 'P' in Philip is soft. The 'T' in Trevor is strong while the 'T' in Theodore is soft. The 'C' in Chelsey is soft, while the 'C' in Carole is strong. The 'e' in Carole differentiates her personality traits significantly from those of Carol without an 'e' at the end of the name. It is accurately defining these very basic differences that help you interpret an individual's traits.

Always keep in mind that even as you go through the process of Name Analysis your subconscious will continually relay semi-subliminal impressions to your conscious mind that you can incorporate into your overall assessment and decision.

FIRST LETTER & LAST LETTER OF THE NAME:

The first and last letters of a person's name denotes how they will initially approach other people and situations. Knowing how someone will inherently act or react can be invaluable in your interactions with them.

A soft letter at the beginning of the name indicates a person who is caring and compassionate, puts others first but also likes to analyze, evaluate and make educated choices and decisions rather than jumping into something without knowledge. A soft letter at the end of the name signifies a person who will always take others into account in all they do and if they feel they are negatively impacting someone else they care about, they may alter their course to accommodate another person's comfort.

Names ending in a soft letter also have the ability to leave things undone or incomplete. They do not have to finish everything they start if they feel what they are doing no longer has significance for them.

People who have a strong letter at the end of their name need to complete all they do. They cannot leave anything undone even if it no longer has value-add for them otherwise they themselves feel incomplete in some way but often can't understand why.

For example, these people will struggle through a poor movie, assuring themselves that it must get better at some point, right until the very end. Once the movie is finished they will then be angry with themselves for allowing the movie to waste two hours of their time. But, they will not be able to turn that movie off part way through. They are 'all or nothing' individuals.

MIDDLE LETTER & ADJACENT MIDDLE LETTERS OF THE NAME:

As mentioned previously, people who have alternating strong and soft or soft and strong letters in their name such as Barbara or Adam are the equalizers, justifiers and peace keepers of the world. Just as their name is the balance between one type of letter and the other like balanced scales so this is their personality. They abhor injustice, discrimination, racism or bias of any kind. They can choose to accept it when directed at them if it is a means to an end however if this imbalance is directed at someone they care about they will go to the greatest degree to regain balance and fairness.

The fewer the letters in a name, the more direct and to the point the individual is. The middle letter is indicative of a person's core strength where life's trials and tribulations are concerned with the adjacent middle letters supporting whether the core of the individual's nature is one of strength or compassion. The outer middle letters give additional meaning to the first and last letters of one's name. For example the name PaT has an 'a' in the middle which is a soft vowel. Therefore Pat's core nature is nurturing, caregiving, compassionate. The 'a' also indicates that she or he would devote their time to making sure others were alright in a crisis and worry about themselves later. The strength of the 'P' and 'T' indicates they would be able to deal with a crisis, trial or tribulation but they will always put others first and worry about themselves later.

The middle letters 'o and r' in the name Lori reflect a very strong core strength, will and determination. When this individual faces a conflict or issue requiring resolve, she will be able to handle it and furthermore will be able to put the issue or situation into perspective, deal with it effectively and carry on. She will never allow herself to be placed in 'victim mode' by another as the very essence of her is too strong willed.

As stated earlier, when we see or hear a name we instantly have first thoughts and impressions. Often when a thought, feeling or impression is that quick to mind and fleeting we brush it aside and disregard it just as we would a cobweb. It is these barely conscious perceptions that can give us our most profound clues, guidance and direction if we pay attention.

Clearly you are not going to take the time to analyze someone's name when you first meet them, and this is not meant to be a crash course in name analysis. However with this bit of basic knowledge when you hear or see someone's name stronger accurate initial impressions will filter through instantly.

In addition to our immediate thoughts, feelings and impressions though, how can we take a name and break it down logically to interpret it and systematically acquire additional information about that individual's character traits? Let's look at a few names and methodically break them down. For easier recognition all STRONG letters will be shown as capital letters, all soft letters will be in lower case and all *dual meaning* letters will be italicized.

Lori:

L	O	R	i
Dual	STRONG	STRONG	soft

L	L reflects that Lori can be strong and determined or flexible and accommodating when approaching a new situation or person. The 'L' also indicates a person who likes to analyze first and make educated choices and decisions rather than impulsively jumping into something or making a snap decision about someone.

O   Again, a strong letter revealing core strength
           and determination to keep going and handle
           any obstacles effectively.

R   Since there are two Strong letters in the middle
           of Lori's name this doubles or magnifies the
           aforementioned traits.

I   The end of Lori's name is a soft letter which
           means she or he doesn't have to finish all they
           start if they feel what they are doing no longer
           has value or purpose for them. This can apply
           to a project, a situation or a person. The 'I'
           also indicates an individual who will always
           take others into consideration with their final
           decisions and if they feel they are impacting
           others negatively, may alter their choices and
           decisions to accommodate those around them
           or may hold fast their choices, depending on
           the circumstances. However they will always
           take that initial time to reflect on their path
           in relation to those around them.

OVERALL: As the name is shorter it also denotes a person
           who usually is direct, doesn't like to beat
           around the bush so to speak and likes to get
           to the point.

EQUAL STRONG & SOFT LETTERS:
(balance, scales of justice)

Nancy:

N	a	N	c	Y
STRONG	soft	STRONG	Dual	STRONG

N	The Strong letter at the beginning of the name reveals a person who sees in 'black and white', there is no grey area in decision making with this letter at the beginning of the name. They are strong, determined and focused on anything they go into with an attitude of 'I will make it work no matter what'.
a	The soft 'a' is this person's caring, compassion and consideration of others. As the 'a' is near the beginning it means that even with the determination to forge ahead, there will always be consideration of others as long as balance is maintained.
N	The 'N' in the middle reflects the core strength and determination to keep going and handle any obstacles effectively, pick themselves up and dust themselves off.
C	The fact that there is one Dual letter toward the end of the name reflects that Nancy also has the characteristics to be stubborn and determined or flexible and accommodating toward the end of her decision making process.

Y   The name Nancy ends with a Strong letter. The strength of this letter adds conviction to all Nancy does, it shows perfectionist traits once choices are made, there is a need to strive to do their best and give their all. The 'Y' also reveals an individual who has to complete all they start otherwise they will feel unsettled and incomplete in some way but not understand why. They will always have to see something to the very end and have closure.

OVERALL: Nancy is the name of balance, like the scales as you have alternating letters between STRONG and soft. As the '*c*' is flanked by two Strong letters indicates regardless of her degree of determination or flexibility with the Dual letter, she will always be steadfast in her decision once it is made and be totally unbending in her choices unless someone gives her an extremely valid reason to change her opinion. As with the scales of justice though, there would have to be equality and balance with the relationship or situation in order for it to be acceptable to someone with this name.

THE DIFFERENCE SPELLING CAN MAKE:

BRIAN VERSUS BRYAN

Brian:

B	R	I	a	N
STRONG	STRONG	soft	soft	STRONG

Bryan:

B	R	Y	a	N
STRONG	STRONG	STRONG	soft	STRONG

Spelling is crucial in determining traits as with the spelling of Brian vs. Bryan above.

Both spellings indicate someone who leads into all they do with determination, conviction and focus. Both ending with the Strong 'N' reflect someone who cannot leave anything undone and has to see all they do through to completion. The two middle letters however change the personality traits significantly as the first spelling with the combined 'i' and 'a' indicates a person whose core trait is the nurturer, caring, compassionate, considerate, warm and giving. This individual will strive to make others comfortable through a crisis and will be what I lovingly refer to as 'the marshmallow inside' meaning they will always put family, friends and those they care about first and foremost and be very open and sharing with their thoughts and feelings. They will put things on hold to accommodate issues of the heart.

The second spelling with the Strong 'Y' in the middle indicates someone who will forge ahead no matter what, at some point take the time to consider those around them and their needs, and as long as everyone seems content enough, will continue to forge ahead with their chosen path, goal, relationship or mission. This is not a negative trait.

For example in a business capacity 'Brian' would take whatever time was needed to make sure everyone else was happy and content even if it was detrimental to critical work or project timelines. Whereas 'Bryan' would take a minute to address those around them but stick with a rigid timeline to complete whatever needed to be done regardless. I would place a Brian in an HR position or a position where timelines were not critical and there was a great degree of flexibility involved. I would also place a 'Brian' in a position where nurturing, caregiving or negotiating and reasoning with others would be an asset but not place him in a position with critical timelines and deadlines unless he was working independently without having to deal with issues or people that could sidetrack him.

In a family or personal situation or a business environment where that warmer compassionate trait is most important, I certainly would rather have a 'Brian' looking after me or my loved ones than a 'Bryan'.

Again, one name and the associated traits are not better than the other. Both fit certain roles better than the other because of their core dispositions.

SHORTENING A NAME:

Shortening a name magnifies the qualities of the name and also means the individual has more of a concise, to the point direct attitude in general.

41

USING A NICKNAME:

A nickname allows the individual to take on the traits associated with the nickname rather than their given name, as the nickname may be more suited to the relationship, person or situation. As an example a football players' given name may be Jake but on the field he's known as Bulldog which is far more aggressive than Jake so sets his energy and vibration to accommodate the fight to win the game.

Initials are also indicative of a different vibration. My father nicknamed our daughter KJ which has the vibrational balance between the Strong 'K' and the soft 'j'.

ALL STRONG LETTERS:

Gordon:

G	O	R	D	O	N
Dual	Strong	Strong	Strong	Strong	Strong

The 'G' is a dual letter which can be Strong or soft however as it has a Strong sound to it (unlike the soft 'G' in George which has a softer, gentler sound). The Strong 'G' indicates a person who goes into all they do with conviction and fortitude. As the 'G' is followed by five more Strong letters and there are no soft letters in the name it reflects someone who is a take charge, get the job done personality. The name also reflects someone who is logical, analytical, likes to make sure all 'I's are dotted and 't's are crossed and see everything through to completion. Gordon can be compassionate when necessary but the matter-of-factness in the name indicates someone who believes you should 'pick yourself up and dust yourself off – stop crying over spilled milk, it's called life so get on with it' attitude. Gordon can have a fun-loving disposition and great sense of humour but the logical analytical side of his personality will always prevail.

If shortened to 'Gord' the conviction, fortitude and analytical nature will be magnified to be even more to the point and concise.

STRONG LETTERS FOLLOWED BY SOFT LETTERS:

OPRAH:

O	P	R	A	H
Strong	Strong	Strong	soft	soft

What of the name of someone famous such as Oprah? The first letter of the name is Strong indicating drive, determination, conviction and fortitude. As the 'O' is followed by two more Strong letters they magnify the qualities of the 'O' but as middle letters themselves also indicate an ability to conquer any challenges or obstacles life throws at her. The third middle letter however is soft indicative of her nurturing, caregiving, compassionate nature and outlook and the soft 'h' at the end of her name shows that she will always take others into account in all she does before she makes her final decision. If she feels she is impacting others negatively she will alter her path to accommodate others – as long as it coincides with her convictions exhibited in the first three letters of her name. The soft 'h' at the end of her name also reveals that she does not have to finish all she starts and if she feels something no longer has 'value add' for her or her situation, she will be able to leave it incomplete and move on to something else.

The name Oprah also indicates someone who loves constant change, constant variety and thrives on things that excite, inspire and motivate her.

Because it is a unique name, not heard very often, it also indicates Oprah is not the leader nor the follower. She is that 'square peg' mentioned earlier who does not fit in the round hole. She will always march to her own drummer and chart her own path as evident by her ongoing success.

PREDOMINANTLY STRONG LETTERS:

Donna:

D   O   N   N   a

At a glance the name Donna starts Strong, ends soft and the core letters in the middle of her name are all Strong. Instantly we know that she will go into all she does with conviction and determination ('D'), have the core strength to handle all challenges and take charge of a situation, has the strength to say 'no' when necessary and has no problem dealing with difficult issues or confrontation ('O', 'N', 'N') yet before completion of anything she does she will take the time to ensure she is not impacting others negatively ('a') and may alter her path to accommodate others depending on her conviction with the particular person or situation at hand. The soft 'a' also reveals she can leave something incomplete if she feels it is no longer significant to her.

PREDOMINANTLY SOFT LETTERS:

Very seldom will you find a full name comprised of soft letters only. Where a name is predominantly soft it will usually have at least one *Dual* meaning letter in it (i.e. Alice, Allissa, Ellie, Cher), which gives the individual that option of being soft or Strong in certain circumstances. Often too, the abbreviated name may have all soft or Strong letters yet the full version has the complimenting soft or Strong letters to bring that yin and yang balance to the personality overall (ie. Jeff / Jeffrey).

SOFT LETTERS ONLY – abbreviated name:

J	e	f	f
Soft	soft	soft	soft

FULL GIVEN NAME:

J	e	f	f	r	e	y
Soft	soft	soft	soft	STRONG	soft	STRONG

In those instances where the name (usually abbreviated or a nickname) has all soft letters such as Jeff it is indicative of a nature that often appears outwardly strong yet the underlying traits are caring, considerate, compassionate, the nurturer and the teacher/educator. Again, teacher/educator does not mean you stand in front of a classroom rather you have a desire to share knowledge with others and help others to enrich themselves in some way. The soft letters also reflect someone who has a shy side to them, can be hurt easily although they may not show it, and more often than not these individuals have a very fun-loving, quirky side to them that makes them seem easy going although they often are very detail-oriented. They can also have a perfectionist streak in them that would have been a result of one or both parents (usually the father figure) setting perfectionist benchmarks for their child/children – especially their sons. (see LIFE TRAITS).

However, the full given name includes two very Strong letters (R, Y). These additional letters give strength, conviction, determination and stubbornness traits to the personality. The 'R' as a middle letter reflects this individuals' ability to handle obstacles and life's problems effectively when necessary and the 'Y' at the end of the name means Jeffrey needs to complete all he starts otherwise he feels incomplete and unsettled. The 'Y' also strengthens the perfectionist, detail oriented traits of the name.

THE STORY OF HANNAH:

Single forty-two year old Hannah felt like the invisible person. She found that people never heard her during conversations to the point where others would simply talk over her. She was soft-spoken, absolutely the nurturer caregiver/teacher educator yet even when she raised her voice for her words to be heard, her words seemed to fall on deaf ears. Although she had many friends and a family who loved her, no one seemed to even be aware of her presence much of the time. She truly felt invisible to others.

The company she had been employed with for many years had recently folded and she was desperate to find work. The only job she was offered was with a collection agency. Though her background was not directly related she was given the task of making those dreaded collections calls to defaulters.

Although a difficult job and not one she was comfortable with, she would always politely introduce herself and company name at the beginning of each call. Not only was she unsuccessful with collecting, most would hang up before she could even initiate a conversation. She knew that unless she started producing results her employment would be short-lived.

Someone jokingly told her she should take on an alias. Why not, she thought. She mulled it over through the weekend, chose a name she felt was powerful and determined and returned to work with an alias and new resolve. She jokingly introduced herself to her employer with her new name. He chuckled, shrugged his shoulders, and told her she could call herself Santa Claus if it got results.

The alias she chose was Monica. The 'MON' at the beginning of the name is incredibly determined, stubborn and confident, the 'c' is a Strong sounding 'c' giving support and additional resolve to the first three letters, while the 'I' and 'a' still gave her the caring, compassion and gentleness to be considerate of other people's situation and misfortune.

She was dumbfounded at how empowered she even felt using the name and by the end of day had positive results from ninety-five percent of the calls she placed. Few hung up on her, most not only listened to all she had to say but responded with the commitment she needed.

'Wow, you're on fire girl!" her employer commented to her as she left that day.

Although she reverted back to Hannah in her personal life, she found that the energy and vibration she carried through the days as Monica left an energy imprint which resulted in those in her 'Hannah' life actually hearing and acknowledging her more than before. Several commented that they had noticed something different about her, not sure what it was, they couldn't put their finger on it, but she was just somehow changed.

As for the traits, energy, and vibration of the name Hannah? The name Hannah has two soft letters at the beginning and two soft letters at the end which are the nurturer/caregiver, teacher/educator traits. Although the double Strong 'N's' in the middle give core strength of character and conviction to handle obstacles, flanked by four soft letters on the outside emitted that gentle, soft, caring, compassionate energy first and foremost. It would be the vibration of the outer four letters that others would interpret initially. Only once others came to know her would they then see the core strength and resolve of her entire character.

WHAT OF DEBORAH AND DARRYL?

D	e	B	O	R	a	h
STRONG	*soft*	*STRONG*	*STRONG*	*STRONG*	*soft*	*soft*

D	a	R	R	Y	l
STRONG	*soft*	*STRONG*	*STRONG*	*STRONG*	*Dual*

Note the similarities between the two names as far as the placement of STRONG versus soft letters. The only difference is the two soft letters at the end of 'Deborah' rather than the singular *Dual* 'l' at the end of Darryl. The Core Traits of Darryl differentiate only slightly with *Dual* 'l' at the end of the name. Darryl would have been the person who could be rigid and stubborn or flexible and caring depending on the person or situation at hand. Whereas Deborah has the double softness of the 'ah' meaning she will always take others into consideration and sometimes alter her path to accommodate those important to her.

So how do you benefit from this basic Name Analysis knowledge?

APPLICATIONS IN YOUR PERSONAL LIFE:

- Is one in the family the 'take charge' personality while the other may need to analyze and evaluate issues to ensure they are making educated decisions;
- Is one the nurturer while the other just likes to 'dust myself off and get on with it';
- Does one need to complete all they start while others can walk away and leave things undone;
- What traits of mine match or conflict with others;
- How do I deal more effectively with family once I understand their natural tendencies;
- Are those around me direct and to the point or do they avoid confrontation or decisions – how do I deal with situations in relation to them;
- How can I guide my children/family more effectively based on their traits and in relation to my traits?

APPLICATIONS IN BUSINESS:

- a power name in a power position;
- a more passive name in a routine or repetitive employee position;
- a direct concise name in a sales position;

- a nurturer in a training capacity;
- a strong yet balanced name in a leadership role;
- a concise, direct, yet need to analyze first name in an accounting position;
- a creative name in a key marketing position, but a creative unique name if a contract position where you want an entrepreneurial spirit;
- an analytical, 'gather all my facts and see the other side of the coin' yet nurturing name in Human Resources.

Just as in a family unit, the weave of personality traits in a business environment can make or break the continuity and success of a company. Therefore not only education, background and experience are essential when considering the appropriate person in the appropriate position, personality trait matching is equally significant. Trait Reading gives you that additional perception to ensure that all relevant aspects of the individual are addressed warranting the best fit for all concerned.

CORE TRAITS SUMMARY:

- The basic interpretation of Core Traits is defined by the sound of the letters and the composition of those letters to create the name.
- Those letters that sound soft indicate a person's gentle, caring, compassionate, considerate nature. Soft letters often are indicative of an individual who is not only the nurturer and caregiver but also the teacher/educator: The person who loves to share their newfound knowledge with the world in some way. This does not mean they go into teaching and stand in front of the class, it means whatever they hear, read or see that

they feel has value they will need to share with those around them.

- Strong letters, just as they sound strong, indicate personal traits that are determined, stubborn, focused and driven.

- Dual letters reflect both soft and strong character traits meaning the individual can be iron-rod rigid or extremely flexible and accommodating depending on the person or issue at hand.

- The first letter of the name indicates how the person approaches other people and situations.

- If the name is unique, the individual's personality will be unique.

- The last letter of the name defines if an individual needs to complete all they start, can leave things undone and the degree of caring and compassion they exert.

- The middle letters reflect the individual's core being, whether that is predominantly caring and compassionate of others foremost, focused driven and determined, or the 'Rock of Gibraltar' for those around them.

- These are the most basic core traits you can analytically discern from the composition of a person's name. Be aware too that as you are analyzing a name those semi-subliminal impressions will continue to filter through. Acknowledge them and incorporate them as they are equally as important.

LIFE TRAITS:

The variables of your Core Traits will always remain basically the same. They are like your backbone and it is your Core Traits that reveal similarities in personalities, such as the example of Barbara earlier.

Your Life Traits are those experiences and interactions with others throughout infancy and childhood that add another subliminal level of energy and vibration to your Core Traits. This additional level defines how you evolve into adulthood; strengthened and forward thinking by your positive and negative experiences or in 'victim' mode from the negatives. These Traits that mould our personality further can also be detected through your subliminal impressions.

Examples of circumstances that contribute to our Life Traits include but are not limited to:

1. Stable loving home environment vs. domineering, controlling parent(s)
2. constant moves or changes throughout childhood vs. environmental stability
3. drugs, alcohol, abuse in the home
4. sibling rivalry vs. sibling connectedness and love
5. popularity vs. lack of through school
6. appropriate praise and encouragement vs. excessive criticism and judgement
7. social and educational structure
8. inter-personal relationships in general

Over the years many people have asked why someone would choose to experience extreme negativity, abuse or poverty rather than a life free of obstacles. In reality all paths have obstacles. They just come in different forms.

It may not be to experience hardship but rather take the challenge of rising above it or creating enough of a ripple to affect positive change on a broader level. Sometimes how we choose to handle our trials and tribulations creates a shift of overall consciousness in the masses such as Terry Fox, Martin Luther King, or Mother Theresa.

You (at your subconscious Level, sometimes referred to as our Soul level) may have chosen to experience a childhood full of abuse to give your abuser the option of veering away from that cruel path and becoming a better person. You may have opted (again at your subconscious level) to go through the abusive process to define your outlook on life in a certain way, chart your career path or choose how you in turn deal with and impact others.

We will all have positive and negative experiences that contribute to our Life Traits however we will always have freedom of choice as to *how* we allow those Traits to define our thoughts, feelings, actions, and consequent energy field and vibration.

Life Trait issues are perceived predominantly through your sensory impressions as you may never be able to validate your impressionistic information about another person's Life Traits but you will sense and feel how their past experiences have defined them.

These thoughts and feelings allow us to be more compassionate or tolerant of traits or behaviour of another. You may never know if the person you are dealing with was abused, abandoned, emotionally smothered by a parent, was popular, unpopular, never felt they had roots since they constantly moved, or loved the constant change and variety frequent moves offered. Where one individual may process an experience negatively, another will embrace that same experience as a positive in their lives.

By making sensory-based assumptions it allows you to justify or excuse traits in another or at least give the benefit of the doubt on one hand but also use those impressions in your determinations.

We have all had cause to say 'I think they've had a hard life', or 'I'll bet they were born with a silver spoon in their mouth.' From a Trait Reading perspective these types of terms are indicative of our immediate yet unsubstantiated first impressions about someone's life versus their personality. We use these phrases all the time yet don't consciously recognize their value to us in our decision-making processes.

BLENDING SENSORY AWARENESS WITH NAME ANALYSIS TO BEGIN BUILDING YOUR TRAIT READING PROFILE

INCORPORATING SENSORY AWARENESS & IMPRESSIONS:

Firstly, let's go back to the beginning and my 'sticky fingers'. Rather than ignore that initial awareness and impression of those two little words, I made a mental note of them while interviewing. As soon as the interview was over I addressed them by simply asking myself what those words meant to me, specifically in relation to the situation at hand, which was the available position and business environment.

My logical interpretation was literally that things would stick to his fingers and as we were in a product-based organization with thousands of items from large to small, it was an ideal setting for someone wanting to steal. Had I been allowed to do my job in this instance, I would have trusted my first thoughts and feelings. I would have rejected his application without taking the hiring process any further. That in turn would have saved the company countless man-hours, police involvement and thousands of dollars in lost revenue.

This is how you incorporate your initial mental/emotional awareness and impressions into your logical/analytical interpretation. You ask what that impression means to you in relation to the person or situation in question. Sometimes we receive what seem to be very random disconnected impressions so we may need a few steps to clarify the meaning for ourselves such as the aroma of bread, which made you think of your mother, which was a wonderful, positive, warm and fuzzy feeling. You would then take the impression of that positive, warm and fuzzy feeling and apply it to whatever you are dealing with or questioning. So the semi-subliminal impressionistic information you are being given is that the outcome of what you are addressing will ultimately be positive and leave you with a warm and fuzzy feeling just like Mom and fresh baked bread. It is like getting a green light to go ahead.

On the contrary, if you receive a negative or upsetting memory or impression you would take that initial sense, apply it to your issue at hand and would probably want to steer clear of the person or situation in question.

I once had a man challenge me about my technique. He was infuriated that I may reject someone based on their name alone and whether I 'liked' that name. As I explained to him it had nothing to do with liking or disliking the name itself. It had to do with what traits a name reveals that may or may not fit the requirements of a position, situation or ability to blend with other individuals. I also emphasized that it was not my only means of deducing information and coming to a final conclusion. He was not pacified and as much as he tried to find fault with my hires and recommendations he could not. He ultimately resigned himself to the rationale that my ability was purely luck and nothing more. I wonder how he would have handled electricity being offered to him in the early 1900's had he lived in that era?

INTERPRETING SYMBOLISM:

Symbolic Sensory Awareness and impressions can be equally telling if we understand how to interpret and apply them. I had a woman attend one of my workshops and through every exercise she only received symbols such as wavy horizontal lines, circles, squares, rectangles and triangles. She felt she was too left-brain oriented as she didn't understand the impressions she was receiving so we broke it down. I asked her to define what she was sensing with each question.

Her first question involved how her business was going to fare over the next six months as it had been struggling recently, to which she received a set of horizontal up and down rolling lines just like waves. I then asked her what those lines meant to her in general. She replied that they meant up and down but not erratic or jagged, there was a smoothness to them. I then asked her to apply that interpretation to her question about her business and apply that same answer based on her interpretation of what the wavy lines meant. "It means my business over the next six months is going to be up and down but there will be a smoothness and pattern to it just like rolling waves," she replied.

Her next question involved her personal growth to which she received the symbol of a triangle. Again, I asked her what a triangle in general meant to her. She replied that she interpreted it to mean a strong solid base and foundation coming to a continual escalation to a peak or point of finality. When she applied it to her question she understood her base to be sound yet her growth would be a steady climb upward, finally culminating in a point of reaching the summit, peak, goal and awareness she would be content with.

Each symbol could be interpreted generally and then applied to her question about a person, their name or a situation she was inquiring about. She also understood how the majority of her hunches, gut feelings and impressions would manifest for her.

ADDING NAME ANALYSIS:

Name Analysis gives you the more practical and analytical means of discerning an individual's core personality and characteristics. You then take the initial hunch/gut feeling impressions you have documented and combine them with your Name Analysis impressions. Keep in mind as you are blending that you may also continue to receive further Sensory Awareness and Name Analysis impressions which should also be noted.

NAME ANALYSIS TRAITS - PROFILE

CORE TRAITS:

GIVEN NAME: __ __ __ __ __ __ __

GOES BY: __ __ __ __ __ __ __

__ __ __ __ __ __ __

ARE THE INDIVIDUAL LETTERS
(STRONG, soft, *Dual*)

FIRST LETTER - MEANING:

_____

_____

_____

LAST LETTER - MEANING:

_____

_____

_____

MIDDLE LETTER - MEANING:

_____

_____

_____

ADJACENT MIDDLE LETTERS - MEANING:

_____

_____

_____

NUMBER OF SYLLABLES – MEANING:

_____

_____

_____

ADDITIONAL SENSORY AWARENESS:

_____

_____

_____

Life Traits are not as easy to discern. Often it is not appropriate to ask someone if they had issues in their childhood or are carrying emotional baggage we should be aware of. Again, as with our first level of information, much of this information will be impressionistic so to simplify the process with the easiest method possible, use the 'yes' or 'no' means of acquiring impressions.

Your concern in a personal relationship or business context is whether an individual may have Life Traits that would have a negative impact on your association with them. As with 'sticky fingers' often you will not be in a position to ask outright however our semi-subliminal impressions once we listen to them will always be validated in some form.

Ask yourself the following:

'Do I sense that (person's name) may have any issues around the following life events that would have a negative impact for me, for my business life, or for the situation at hand?' Go with your very first hunch, thought or gut feeling. Don't worry about being right or wrong, as this is for your information and use only. Check the Positive or Negative column which generates the strongest immediate thoughts, feelings and impressions you receive. If there are other areas you need to inquire about use the 'Other' sections at the bottom of the table.

POSITIVE INFLUENCES	☑	NEGATIVE INFLUENCES	☑
Stable loving home environment		Domineering, controlling parent(s)	
Environmental stability		Constant moves or changes in childhood	
Substance/abuse free home		Drugs, alcohol, abuse in the home	
Sibling respect & love		Sibling rivalry & jealousy	
Popularity in school		Bullying, not well liked or accepted	
Appropriate praise and encouragement		Excessive criticism and judgement	
Positive social and educational structure		Negative social and educational structure	
Strong and solid inter-personal relationships in general		Negative or weak inter-personal relationships in general	
Other:		Other:	
Other:		Other:	
Other:		Other:	
Other:		Other:	

ADDITIONAL SENSORY AWARENESS & IMPRESSIONS:

_____

_____

_____

_____

_____

_____

_____

_____

_____

_____

_____

_____

_____

_____

_____

_____

_____

_____

_____

_____

_____

_____

_____

_____

_____

_____

_____

Part 3

LEVEL 3

BRAIN WIRING TRAITS

(What Our Most Basic Words & Actions Reveal)

Just as the traits from Sensory Awareness and understanding of Name Analysis can be interpreted by others, so can our Brain Wiring traits through our very actions and the words we speak. This is the last Level or means of acquiring Trait information about another that is relevant to Trait Reading and although some of this information was covered in my previous book entitled 'Discover the Magic' it is relevant to individual personality traits where Trait Reading is concerned.

As we covered previously in Parts 2 & 3, our Sensory Awareness and Name Analysis reveals the energy/vibrational and mental/ emotional qualities of us. To take this one step further, *what* we do and *how* we say things divulges how our brain is wired. As with the choir, tuning fork, and resulting vibration and energy field, your unique brain wiring also defines how effectively you may or may not interact with those around you. And although we are covering the very basics of Brain Wiring, it is always the simplicities that define traits most accurately.

Our Brain Wiring defines the following in us. If we are:

- Left-brain, Right-brain, or Whole-brain;
- Positive or Negative Processor;
- See in Black and White or Grey;
- Builder or Maintainer,
- Giver or Taker;
- Teacher / Educator

Identifying these traits and their unique vibration in relation to yours significantly increases your ability to interact more effectively and Trait Read more concisely.

In relation to Name Analysis Left-brain individuals will tend to have more strong letters in their name than soft and usually strong letters at the beginning of their name. Right-brain individuals will tend to have a majority of soft letters in their name which not only depicts their nurturing, caring compassionate traits but also their creative side. Whole-brain individuals will as a general rule tend to have a balance of strong and soft letters, much like the scales as we have discussed earlier.

Stronger letters also tend to indicate that an individual will see more in Black and White than Grey, will be more the Builder than the Maintainer and have a tendency to be more the Taker rather than the Giver.

Softer letters generally represent the more creative traits, often more Right-Brain or Whole-Brain, see in Grey rather than Black and White, can be the Builder or the Maintainer, is usually more of a Giver than Taker, and will have strong Teacher/Educator qualities. Always keep in mind that these are general interpretations and extreme life traumas or negative experiences can change one's energies to such a great degree that the original Name and associated Core traits may no longer fit their altered personality. This is often when we see a radical name change of some form as discussed earlier.

Positive and Negative Processor Traits are somewhat harder to discern through Name Analysis as it is usually the individuals' words and actions that allow us to discern their Brain Wiring traits as explained later in this section.

APPLICATIONS IN YOUR PERSONAL & BUSINESS LIFE

YOUR PERSONAL LIFE:

How is the interpretation of all traits applicable in your personal life? Understanding Sensory Awareness, Name Analysis, and Brain Wiring traits gives you a deeper recognition of what makes others tick; especially in relation to you. It allows you to justify differences rather than resisting or resenting them. It also allows you to interact more effectively without the need for others to 'open up' to you. When you have a sense of where someone else is coming from semi-subliminally it allows you to gauge your actions and reactions more appropriately to gain the outcome and results you want and need. Information acquired with the three Levels gives you added insight and awareness in such areas as:

- is this the right relationship for me;
- where is the other person coming from emotionally;
- can I trust this person;
- what traits of mine match or conflict with theirs;

- how do I interact more effectively knowing these traits, similarities, and differences;
- how do I help others in my family interact better to minimize conflict in the home;
- how can I direct my children effectively in their choices and decisions about career paths, relationships, health and wellness?

APPLICATIONS IN BUSINESS:

How is Trait Reading applicable to the work environment? By ensuring the most appropriate personality coincides with their corporate position. For example:

- power name in a power position;
- a more passive name in a routine or repetitive employee position;
- a taker in a sales position;
- a giver in a training capacity;
- a builder in a leadership role;
- a left-brain in an accounting position except at a Controller or Comptroller level in which case you want also want a builder;
- a right-brain in a key marketing position, not a left-brain;
- a grey in Human Resources, not a black & white.

CONSCIOUS PERCEPTIONS OF BRAIN WIRING TRAITS

Just as our subconscious interprets the Core and Life traits of an individual by their Name that we can utilize, we simultaneously receive those conscious perceptions of another's character based on their physical words, actions and mannerisms. By understanding the very basic brain wiring of an individual as well allows us to quickly discern similarities and differences between us and them. These differences can then be understood, respected and appreciated in another rather than being a source of frustration, annoyance or resentment.

Life traits as revealed by a Name can shift depending on life experiences. However, an individuals' Brain Wiring traits and way of perceiving, as well as their Core personality traits cannot be changed. These Traits are inherent in the individual from birth to death. We cannot change someone else's Wiring nor our own, however once we recognize *how* someone else is wired we can alter our method of communicating with them to accommodate their wiring if we choose to.

THE BOARD OF DIRECTORS:

Several years ago a client complained to me about a key member of the Board of Directors she was Chairing. She expressed that this individual was so incredibly detail-oriented, logical, analytical, picky and petty, that she was driving the other Board members to distraction with her constant questions. I asked about the professions of the other Board members and learned they were all connected to the arts in some fashion.

"So most on your Board are very creative?" I then asked.

"Very much so", was the response I received.

The frustrating key member in question was a bookkeeper whom they had appointed as Treasurer. The other members felt with her bookkeeping abilities nothing would fall through the cracks and no other member wanted such a detail-oriented repetitive task.

I inquired if anyone on the Board was taking the time to answer this woman's questions but apparently all were so frustrated they no longer acknowledged her questions, and for the most part ignored her completely.

I pointed out to my client that clearly their Treasurer, just by her very questions and actions was left-brain oriented. Absolutely a trait you want in that position. I then explained that the other Board members were more right-brain inclined as apparent with their professions. As far as the right-brain members were concerned they always gave their Treasurer the information she needed however for their Treasurer it was never sufficient; hence the frequent questioning.

I explained how left-brain people do tend to frustrate right-brain people and vice versa but they had assigned this woman to the position of Treasurer because they knew how meticulous she was. They wanted the perfectionist in that role to ensure all the 'i's were dotted and the 't's were crossed so to speak. Yet when this left-brain oriented woman tried to do her job efficiently, she was met with resistance since right-brain individuals become frustrated by the smaller details so critical to running a business properly.

For example a right-brain individual will submit a receipt identifying 'when'. A left-brain individual such as this bookkeeper would need to know the 'when', 'where', 'why', and 'how' connected to that receipt. The Board members were also viewing their Treasurers' questions as constantly challenging and interrogating as if they were guilty or being deceitful, putting them on the defensive and ultimately avoiding her. All their Treasurer was trying to do was gain the facts she required to ensure her records were complete. Therein was the miscommunication and ensuing frustration for all parties.

"I never thought of it that way" she replied. "We wanted her in that role because of the very traits we are frustrated with... we just assumed with her background she would have all the answers." She began to smile. "Now I understand."

The Chairperson not only began working more tolerantly with her Treasurer but also took the time to enlighten the other Board Members as to the differences in wiring that were the root of their frustrations. The last I heard, this Board of Directors was humming along beautifully.

The concept of left-brain, right-brain and whole-brain has been around for a few decades but I would like to present how your awareness of it from a different perspective as with the previous story, can be beneficial to you when dealing with others. Bear in mind too that people will always have minor elements of all traits, which are evident from time to time. However what we are doing is looking at the dominant traits they display the majority of the time which we can identify and utilize.

LEFT-BRAIN, RIGHT-BRAIN, WHOLE-BRAIN:

(On a vibrational level 90% of the population are either left or right-brain; only 10% are whole brain. Respect the differences)

Left-Brain: Logical, analytical, detailed, academic, needs to have everything organized, makes lists, often perfectionists, need to control. (E.g. Accountants, Lawyers, Investors, Bankers). Will be candid and to the point in their conversations and have no time for those who they feel are long-winded and descriptive. Their words and actions will be concise, matter of fact and direct to the situation or conversation at hand. Left-Brain individuals will often be more Black and White in their outlook and decisions.

Right-Brain: Artistic, creative, goes with the flow, doesn't like answering to authority (Artists, Musicians, Designers, Marketing, Advertising). Right-Brain individuals usually don't make lists, tend to see situations more as Grey and have the ability to see other options or 'the other side of the coin'. Tend to have a more spontaneous, adventurous side and like to bend the rules or not follow them at all. Often entrepreneurial but may lack the logical left-brain traits to run a business effectively therefore needing someone of more left or whole-brain persuasion to handle that area for them.

Whole-Brain: Not extreme left or right traits, a balance of both indicated above but neither to excess, needs to work in an area that accommodates both their logical analytical nature and their creativity (Engineers, IT, Architects, Producers.)

Personal Relevance:

If you have two Right-Brain individuals or two Left-Brain individuals they will be more on the same 'wavelength' whereas a Left-Brain and a Right-Brain together will be like two ships passing in the night. They may be on the same ocean so to speak but miles apart in their outlook and methodologies. They will frustrate each other to no end unless they are aware and respectful of the others' characteristics.

Business Relevance:

Placing a Right-Brain creative individual into a Left-Brain position such as accounting where detail is paramount would be disastrous for the company and lead to failure for the individual. A Whole-Brain person would function effectively in an IT position where new applications are constantly required. They would effectively couple their Left-Brain analytical skills with their Right-Brain creative abilities to generate the desired results. A Left-Brain could not successfully sustain a Right-Brain role such as advertising unless they were involved solely in the research area rather than the creative aspect.

Forty Years of Left-Brain vs. Right-Brain:

A Left-Brain individual often views a Right-Brain person as 'flighty', 'illogical', 'scattered', artsy. A Right-Brain person views a Left-Brain as 'detailed', 'picky', 'petty', 'controlling' as the Left-Brain individual usually likes things done their way.

My husband is a whole-brain individual with predominantly left–brain tendencies. I definitely am right-brain. We have been together forty years and throughout that entire time he has insisted that the toilet paper roll needs to go on a certain way, which for those of you who don't know, is over the top. The Right-Brain person is just happy the toilet paper is there.

Several years ago my husband complained that there was a conspiracy in our household and that my daughter and I were intentionally placing the toilet paper rolls the other way just to irritate him. Unbeknownst to all of us, our cleaners who also knew of his pet peeve, were reversing the rolls each time they came to clean, just for the fun of it. Although he eventually saw the humour in it, initially he was not amused.

Left-Brain people also love to make lists while right-brains usually just wing it. Again, for the last forty years my husband will make a shopping and errand list, then hand me the list. Why on earth would you give a right-brain individual a list? Ninety–nine percent of the time I would have left the list at home or misplaced it by the time we reached our first destination. Hence the disagreement would begin. I would suggest to him that since it was his list he should have been responsible for it and since he made the list surely he must remember what he put on it. His reply would always be that if he could remember he wouldn't have to make a list now would he. Ah the traits of an old married couple.

My husband always wanted the toothpaste squeezed from the bottom not from the middle. For years I would squeeze from the middle (my hands are smaller), replace the cap and then work the toothpaste up from the bottom to appease him. We now have two tubes of toothpaste, his and hers. He squeezes his from the bottom and I squeeze mine from the middle. These are very little idiosyncrasies in themselves insignificant. However, over time they may be major irritants if you don't recognize each others' wiring. They can become the 'why can't you just do it my way' scenarios.

Left-brain students exceed scholastically since our school system is designed to accommodate predominantly left-brain thinking. Right-brain students often feel inferior in this environment. Although one is no brighter than the other overall, the system is geared to accentuate left-brain abilities. As adults it is frequently the right-brain individual whose successes far surpass those of their left-brain peers.

One isn't better or brighter than the other, just wired differently.

Usually it will be the left-brain individual who will strive to 'educate' and 'instil' their logical thought processes into their right-brain affiliate. A common phrase of a left-brain individual; "it's only common sense", or "it's only logical", or "why would you do that, what were you thinking, where is your brain".

The right-brain may respond by shrugging the attempts off, become defensive or verbally aggressive if they feel they are being judged or criticized, or subservient if their self-esteem is already diminished to a certain point.

POSITIVE vs. NEGATIVE PROCESSORS:

Again relating to individual 'wiring', every person is either a 'Positive Processor' or 'Negative Processor' type personality. A Positive Processor digests information and experiences in one fashion while a Negative Processor assimilates much differently.

One isn't better than the other, however from early childhood, how praise and criticism is delivered to these two personality types is paramount in creating strong, well-developed self-worth or destroying it.

The Positive Processor: Accepts motivational criticism easily, will use it to advance themselves personally and career-wise, you can mix praise with criticism and it will be received as intended.

The Negative Processor: Possesses a sensitive nature, holds emotions and feelings in, cannot accept criticism or a 'but' coupled with praise, will become quiet, sullen, withdrawn or suddenly argumentative and will hear only the negative not the positive. Their self-esteem is easily impacted, will blossom instantly with praise. If critique is necessary use

an indirect method such as
giving an example similar to
their situation rather than a
direct criticism.

Why Does One Child 'Blossom' While Another One 'Wilts':

Assume for a moment that you have two children. Unbeknownst to you one is a Positive Processor the other a Negative Processor. Both try their best at school; both proudly come home with 'B's on their report cards. They excitedly hand their report cards over to you.

Thrilled with their marks you make exactly the same statement to both:

"Congratulations! We're so proud of you! You got a 'B'! **But,** if you can get a 'B', you can get an 'A'."

It is a very simple statement delivered by the loving parent with praise and motivational enthusiasm. The Positive Processor will respond enthusiastically to your words and beam with pride.

The Positive Processor will hear the message exactly as intended, recognize the praise and view the 'but' as a goal to strive for since their parent believes in them.

The Negative Processor will not even hear the praise and will interpret the motivational 'but' as criticism and judgement. They will assume they failed in their parent's eyes. The Negative Processor's adverse reaction is confusing to the parent who truly believes they have just praised and motivated both children.

It is imperative that the Negative Processor receives praise without the motivationally intended 'but' as the motivational part of the statement will negate all praise leaving the child feeling they fell short and failed.

Misinterpreting they have been criticized, the Negative Processor will instantly become despondent, sullen, withdrawn and depending on the degree of frustration and anger, may be aggressive or sarcastic. They will feel they have fallen short of expectations, creating a 'why even bother trying when my best isn't good enough anyway' attitude.

The Negative Processor will not strive to better themselves, fearful of failing again in their parent's eyes. They will subconsciously adopt an achievement level of acceptable mediocrity. This ensures they would not raise expectations and benchmark but also would not fail, which would bring more criticism. They create a pattern of just doing an acceptable job or attaining an average mark, coasting through as unnoticed as possible.

If a parent intentionally criticizes passively or aggressively, bordering on verbal abuse the child's esteem will diminish significantly enough to result in addictions of some form.

If the parent provides only praise and omits the '**but**' component of the sentence, the Negative Processor will strive for the 'A' or higher goal secretly in case they don't succeed. If the remark is intentionally critical the Negative Processor will internalize it and adopt a victim mindset.

As the parent sees their Negative Processor child's self-esteem plummeting they try harder to motivate unaware that their very words are inadvertently diminishing their child's self-confidence further. The harder they parent tries, the more frustrated, angry and withdrawn the child becomes over the misperceived criticisms and admonishments. Hence it creates a 'catch 22' scenario.

The parent rationalizes by stating 'they don't understand since they deal with both children exactly the same way'. Therein lies the problem – both children are not exactly the same therefore they need to be spoken to differently.

A Negative Processor (especially teen or young adult) will also misinterpret any advice, guidance and opinions you put forward as yet again judging, criticizing them and trying to control their life (just so you know).

These reactions pertain to any age group and the aforementioned scenarios can apply to any interaction from parent to child; employer to employee; husband to wife; to friends, family and co-workers.

Business Relevance:

Ideally an organization strives to employ as many positive individuals as possible however many do function successfully from a negative position. To work effectively with the negative personality praise constantly, (when warranted), criticize minimally. NEVER combine praise with critique. The critique will obliterate the praise leaving the individual feeling they missed the 'benchmark' and failed.

A Negative Processor responds oppositely to motivational tactics such as "Great job Bob, you landed that sale, BUT if you landed that one you could land all of them." What the Negative Processor will digest is the 'BUT...' portion of the statement, the 'Great...' segment is all but lost on a Negative Processor. Their immediate non-verbal action is usually one of quietness, sullenness, despondence, occasionally aggressive or sarcastic, leaving the deliverer confused since the message was meant to be congratulatory and motivational in nature.

A Positive Processor will hear the message exactly as it is intended, take it as a pat on the back and recognition of a goal to strive for since someone else believes in their ability to succeed.

Personal Relevance:

Apply the same Business Relevance to your home environment, friends and family. Identify who is Positive, who is Negative and respect the unique wiring each possesses. If you give praise only without a criticizing or motivating 'but', both Positive and Negative Processors will mentally and emotionally 'blossom'.

The Positive/Negative Processor experiences throughout childhood can also be detected in one's Life traits as discussed previously.

BLACK & WHITE OR GREY:

Black & White: Sees the world as either/or, right/wrong, good/bad, success/failure – no middle ground, very definite outlook on life, and very strong stubborn viewpoint, can change their position but only if given strong, justifiable reasons.

Grey: Always see the 'other side of the coin' or someone else's point of view and needs to gather all of the facts before making a decision. In extreme cases however a Grey may be unable to make a decision and will be the consummate 'follower' or 'maintainer' content to follow decisions, guidance and directions from another.

Business Relevance:

Anyone in a strong decision-making role should be a Black & White. Roles requiring the ability to 'see both sides of the coin', negotiating, arbitrating or constantly communicating and liaising should be occupied by those of Grey disposition.

Personal Relevance:

Grey individuals will be very frustrated with the 'cut and dried', 'just make a decision now' mindset of the Black and White individual, whereas the Black and White has difficulty dealing with the Grey personalities' need to weigh, analyze, and study all facets before making a decision.

BUILDER OR MAINTAINER:

(10% are Builders, 90% are Maintainers)

Builder: A Builder needs to create something from nothing, loses interest once building is done, needs constant change and variety and is a visionary. Co-workers, friends and family will often criticize the Builder as they feel the Builder is never satisfied. The Builder often becomes frustrated if, once they reach their goal, they inadvertently slide to a Maintainer role as they cannot 'baby-sit'. Therefore a Builder needs one of three things to happen to position them back into their natural Trait of Builder mode:

1. move to a new goal-driven venue
2. sell in the case of self-employment and start a new venture
3. put in a Maintainer and oversee only, while they take on a new venture.

Maintainer: The Maintainer is happiest maintaining and falls in behind the Builder. The Maintainer is exceptional at maintaining status quo, likes security, will always let a Builder take the risks, and enjoys routine. Fearful of change, a Maintainer will try to keep everything around them constant.

Maintainers are usually detail-oriented, often perfectionists and feel a great sense of satisfaction in supporting a Builder as the role they play usually provides the integral backbone and structure to what a Builder is creating.

Builders are the inventors and creators of the world. They not only don't think inside the box, they don't even know a box exists. They need constant change and constant variety. They, become bored very quickly, and once bored become despondent, frustrated and cranky.

A Builders' need for change unsettles a Maintainer, therefore a Maintainer will try to alter the Builders traits to conform more with theirs in order to give the Maintainer a sense of comfort. A Builder on the other hand usually views the Maintainer as 'security conscious', cautious and limited.

Builders need to embrace their inherent characteristic and accommodate it if they are to be happy. Maintainers need to recognize and respect it. By the same token, Builders need to understand that their changes cause actual anxiety for those who are Maintainers. To pacify a Maintainer, a Builder needs to constantly reassure the Maintainer that all is going well.

Builders need to remember that once their goal has been attained, they unintentionally become the Maintainer, a role in which they become despondent and frustrated unless they can source out a new direction that excites, inspires and motivates them.

Builder Child with Maintainer Parent(s):

For a Builder child in a Maintainer parented
household, the parents will inadvertently
undermine any Builder tendencies their child
displays with negative or dissuading comments.
This causes the Builder child to second-guess
their own decision-making abilities. The advice
also causes inner conflict as the Builder child
trusts their parents' guidance, and wishing to
please, will minimize or eliminate their Builder
traits to shadow their parents' beliefs and desires.

The Maintainer parent expounds their negatives
truly believing they are saving their child from
disappointment and failure. What they are
actually doing is inadvertently placing their
own Maintainer fears and apprehensions onto
their Builder child to keep that child safe,
sound and happy – by Maintainer standards and
benchmarks.

Maintainer Child with Builder Parent(s):

A Maintainer child in a Builder parented
household will struggle as the parents try to
pull their child out of their natural Maintainer
comfort zone of following and supporting
another. The Maintainer child will feel
insecure and unable to come up to the parent's
expectations and benchmarks. A strong
domineering Builder parent may try to force
their Maintainer child into becoming a Builder

regardless. Although not intended, this pressure sets their child up to fail if the child succumbs in order to gain parental approval. This is often where the Maintainer child resorts to alcohol or drugs in an attempt to escape the excessive pressure of trying to achieve the benchmark set by the parent(s).

A BUILDER FATHER'S DREAMS, A MAINTAINER SON'S AMBITIONS

From the day his only child Will was born, rugged six-foot four Tom dreamed of passing his legacy and construction business on to his son. A dream Tom pushed on Will constantly throughout his son's childhood. As his son grew into adulthood however it became clear to Tom that Will wasn't interested in the family business at all. Tom wanted his son to play hockey as he had as a child, but again Will didn't have the slightest interest in that sport or any other. Although Tom couldn't find fault with his son's grades, particularly the maths and sciences, he longed to do 'guy' things with Will.

As Will entered his teens Tom, hoping to inspire and coerce, offered him a part time job at his company and began pressuring him to become involved in the business after graduating. Tom dreamed of his son one day taking over and running the Company. Although Will was appreciative of the job and future opportunity, he announced to his parents that he was set on becoming a nurse.

Tom was devastated. How could his son want to go into such a profession – a doctor yes – but a nurse – not construction?

Tom thought of the comments and teasing he would hear from friends and family.

Will was determined to follow his own path even though his father made his disappointment very clear. Will graduated from Nursing with Honours and gained a nursing position immediately. He is contentedly working as a team member under a large umbrella in a Maintainer role.

Over time Tom came to accept and respect Will's choice. He also came to realize that for all those years it was only his dream to have his son working with him. Will had always had goals of his own and the courage to follow them in spite of his father's wishes.

Business Relevance:

An individual who thrives on routine is usually exceptional in a Maintainer support role, but should never be moved into a Builder position. Builders are visionaries, strong, determined, and decisive. Unless a Maintainer evolves into and displays Builder characteristics, a Maintainer should always remain in a Maintainer position. To put a Maintainer in a Builder position often leads to health and stress management issues, and burnout for the Maintainer. The Executive or Builder who positioned them will constantly be frustrated and feel they have to 'carry' that employee or micro-manage with ongoing direction to get the job done.

Personal Relevance:

Usually a Builder will hear phrases from family, friends and co-workers such as 'why aren't you ever satisfied'; 'you finally reached your goal and it still isn't enough for you'; 'when is good enough good enough'. Maintainers will go to great lengths to dissuade Builders from forging ahead, often validating their position with reasons why the Builders' plans could fail. This is often perceived by the Builder as lack of trust and support, when if fact the Maintainer is inadvertently placing their own fears, apprehensions and insecurities onto the Builder.

In a personal Builder/Maintainer relationship both need to recognize and respect the other's traits otherwise the relationship will constantly have an underlying 'tug of war' energy to it. Ultimately one will be forced to either alter their natural traits in order to keep the relationship, or leave the relationship entirely.

Like Positive/Negative Processor Brain Wiring, Builder/ Maintainer interactions throughout youth can create significant Life traits.

GIVER OR TAKER:

Giver: Always does for others, team player, nurturer, caregiver, teacher, educator, sometimes to their own detriment; ignores their needs to accommodate others.

Taker: Monetarily based, watches out for best personal scenario, will have limited loyalty, always go with the best offer, driver, determined, focused, can masquerade as giver to get what they want, will always have ulterior motive when giving.

Business Relevance:

A Giver requires a position where nurturing, care giving, teaching, educating is expected. To put a Giver into a Sales position for example would result in the individual 'giving away the farm' when negotiating with customers or clients. A Taker is paramount in a sales position since their drive, determination to maximize both their bottom line and that of the company, will be first and foremost.

To place a Taker in a Human Resources position would lead to disruption for the employee and management since a Taker's primary role is to satisfy his/her needs foremost, depending on which worked to best advantage. A Taker generally sees in Black & White, with an inability to see the Grey areas often required for conflict resolution.

Personal Relevance:

An ideal relationship is a Giver with a Giver. A Giver/Taker relationship will only survive as long as the Giver gives unconditionally. If the Giver tires of giving and not receiving sufficiently in return from the Taker, the Giver will begin to demand reciprocity which does not work for a Taker. The negative dynamics will escalate until the Taker makes life so difficult for the Giver, the Giver will leave the relationship. This allows the Taker to 'claim' the 'victim' role in the relationship thereby attracting a new Giver. Takers are NEVER drawn to each other.

TEACHER &   Always needs to impart wisdom, knowledge,
EDUCATOR: information to those around them whether part of their job specifications or not and will often leave their own work to accommodate educating someone having difficulty.

Business Relevance:

A Teacher/Educator is a tremendous asset to the workplace in roles such as Human Resources, Supervisory capacities, middle – upper management sales and marketing (depending on the corporate structure) as the greater the knowledge, the sounder the base. You do not want a Teacher/Educator in a general worker/maintainer role, as they will constantly divert their attention from their own work to educate and assist those around them, whether requested or not.

Personal Relevance:

Sometimes a Teacher/Educator provides welcome knowledge and information but often they expound constantly giving the impression of being the know-it-all.

TRAIT POSITIONING IN A CORPORATE ENVIRONMENT:

The following chart indicates the traits that would be most desirable in key corporate positions. These can vary depending on the criteria of the position and type of business however as a general rule these would be the primary traits I would seek for each position.

Always remember that one trait is no better or lesser than another. Each trait on its own merit rounds out and completes an individual as they are meant to be, and each trait provides the associated attributes most desirable to the situation at hand.

Take a minute and note the individuals around you. How do they fit into the categories and how effective are they in their present roles and in conjunction with those around them.

Are there any circumstances where it is glaringly obvious that one's traits are mismatched to their position or current situation? Which traits would have been more desirable for the position or situation and where would that individual and those traits possibly be better suited?

I have used the example as it pertains to business however this chart can be applied to any area of your life; whether that is education, personal or self-employment. Who do you interact with on a regular basis? Use the charts, define their traits in relation to their status and in relation to you. Note areas where you are in sync and areas where you are not. Embrace the similarities and respect and appreciate the differences.

Where you feel more than one trait is relevant make a note of it but wherever possible try to discern what would be the primary dominant trait with a strong secondary trait that applies in certain circumstances. Clearly everyone is a combination of traits to a degree and no one will slot perfectly into all categories but that's what makes all of us so uniquely individual. What you are looking for is predominant only as a means of understanding others better and benefiting you and them with this understanding.

BUSINESS ENVIRONMENT – PREDOMINENT POSITIONS – DESIRED BRAIN WIRING TRAITS:

Although there are always exceptions depending on the company dynamics, these are the predominant desirable traits per position.

NAME/ TITLE	POSITIVE or NEGATIVE	LEFT BRAIN, RIGHT BRAIN, WHOLE BRAIN	BUILDER or MAINTAINER	GIVER or TAKER	TEACHER, EDUCATOR	BLACK & WHITE or GREY
CEO / PRESIDENT	Positive	Left/Whole Brain	Builder	Taker	No	Black & White
VP SALES	Positive	Left-Brain	Builder	Taker	Yes	Grey
VP MARKETING	Positive	Right/Whole Brain	Builder	Taker	Yes	Black & White
VP FINANCE	Positive	Left Brain	Builder	Taker	No	Black & White
VP H.R.	Positive	Whole Brain	Maintainer	Giver	Yes	Grey
MANAGER	Positive	Left Brain	Maintainer	Taker	No	Grey
SUPERVISOR	Positive	Left Brain	Maintainer	Giver	Yes	Grey
ASSOCIATE	Positive	Position Dependent	Maintainer	Giver	No	Grey

BRAIN WIRING TRAITS - PROFILE

BRAIN WIRING ANALYSIS SHEET

GIVEN NAME: _____ GOES BY: _____

AGE: (approx. if possible) _____

PREDOMIENT BRAIN WIRING TRAIT	✓	POSITION &/OR RELATIONSHIP TO YOU	ADDITIONAL IMPRESSIONS
LEFT BRAIN			
RIGHT BRAIN			
WHOLE BRAIN POSITIVE PROCESSOR			
NEGATIVE PROCESSOR			
BLACK/WHITE			
GREY			
BUILDER			
MAINTAINER			
GIVER			
TAKER			
TEACHER			
EDUCATOR			

ADDITIONAL SENSORY AWARENESS & IMPRESSIONS:

Part 4

PROFILE SUMMATION

PULLING IT ALL TOGETHER
SUMMATION OF LEVELS 1, 2 & 3

Review the information you have gathered from each section; the beginning with your immediate impressions and Sensory Awareness; the characteristics and traits of Name Analysis as defined by the Core and Life traits; and the final Level with Brain Wiring traits.

Make any additional notes you feel are relevant to the individual (or situation if reviewing the name of a place, business, investment, etc.).

Lastly, set the Trait Reading Profile aside and proceed with your normal logically-based process of discerning information. Once that process is complete, blend the two modes of information together and formulate your final decision.

IN CLOSING:

The areas we have covered are very broad general categorizations and tools designed to raise your awareness and hone your abilities to perceive. As you expand your awareness and practice this technique of Trait Reading and profile building you ultimately will be able to accurately Trait Read a person, place, thing or situation within 10 seconds. Over time you will discover you no longer need the step by step process as the necessary information will come to you instinctively – just like 'sticky fingers'.

Listen to yourself and those around in a whole new way. Embrace your newfound knowledge and perceptions. Give yourself the edge by exercising your inherent abilities with three new Levels of recognition, understanding and insight. Use the information you acquire wisely and for the betterment of yourself, your choices and decisions, your life, and for the enrichment of your relationships with others.

Part 5

ABOUT THE AUTHOR, BOOKS, PROGRAMS AND SERVICES

SPEAKING ENGAGEMENTS:

Deborah is a widely sought after Key Note Speaker. Depending on your venue Deborah's topics can cover but are not limited to...

- Trait Reading Others Effectively Personally & Professionally
- Mind Set, Go – Creating Your Reality
- Communication & Inter-personal Relationships
- Health and Wellness
- Understanding & Relating To Our Youth More Effectively
- Mediumship and Reaching Out to Those We Have Lost

...all from a refreshingly new energy-based perspective.

Each speaking engagement can be customized to suit your needs, from a 30 or 60 minute Key Note Presentation at your AGM to a two-day Workshop intensive for your staff or group.

Deborah's books in her Series 'The Deborah Johnson Series' available for purchase:

- **NEW – TRAIT READER**
- **NEW – MIND SET, GO!**
- **DISCOVER THE MAGIC**
- **LOOK WITHIN, HEAL WITHOUT**

ABOUT:

- **TRAIT READER:**
  What Traits Do Your Very Name, Your Energy, Your Mannerisms, Words & Actions Reveal About You? What Traits Do Others Reveal That You Can Benefit From? How Can You Use This Knowledge For Greater Success in Business and Your Personal Life?

- **TRAIT READER TRAINING PROGRAM:**
  If you are interested in developing your Trait Reading skills to a greater degree please e-mail Deborah at deborah@deborahjohnson.ca for information about her Beginner, Intermediate and Master Level training programs.

- **MIND SET, GO!:**
  Discover the KIS Principle of Fulfilling Your Life, Fulfilling Your Goals, Fulfilling Your Dreams with such a Simple Straight-forward Mindset, anyone can successfully adopt it and reap the benefits.

- **DISCOVER THE MAGIC:**
  Three-time International Award Winning 'Discover the Magic' received International recognition in the Los Angeles International Book Awards winning in 'New Age Non-Fiction' and 'Social Change' categories. Discover the Magic was also named one of the best reads of 2011 by 'USA Best Books of 2011'. Discover the Magic gives you the knowledge and tools to understand yourself better and communicate with others more effectively.

- **LOOK WITHIN, HEAL WITHOUT:**
  Look Within, Heal Without is an Exercise/Metaphysical Awareness Stretching program. Through 20 minutes a day of simple physical stretching and breathing coupled with an understanding of how our emotions contribute to our overall wellness, we can regain greater control over own health and well-being. Testimonials state that this easy routine has proven to be incredibly successful with weight loss, lowering high blood pressure and even improving one's golf game significantly!

PRIVATE SESSIONS:

All of Deborah's sessions are either ½ hour or 1 hour in length and are done by phone or skype. This mode of communicating allows Deborah's clients to be able to reach her from anywhere in the world and benefit from her services. To arrange an individual session:
email <u>deborah@deborahjohnson.ca</u>.

BIOGRAPHY

deborah
johnson
VISIONARY COACH AUTHOR SPEAKER

Author and Keynote Speaker, Deborah Johnson is an Internationally-known personal and corporate Visionary, Medium, and Inspirational Motivator focused on Esteem and Empowerment. Deborah utilizes over 20 years' experience to coach, instruct and direct others to move past their blocks and achieve their full potential.

Deborah works with clients from all walks seeking guidance and direction in their lives. She also works extensively with corporate clients offering an esteem and empowerment based venue which dovetails effectively with traditional business practices.

A well-known TV and radio personality who has been featured in numerous books and magazines, Deborah brings her enthusiasm, integrity and extensive knowledge to her clients as she invites, inspires, and motivates her diverse client base to strive beyond the limitations they have set for themselves.

Deborah's newly-released 2-Book Series and related Programs 'Trait Reader' and 'Mind, Set, Go!' gives the reader two new venues of awareness. Her previous books 'Discover The Magic' and 'Look Within, Heal Without' are available for added insight.

Through her workshops and seminars Deborah trains and coaches individuals and groups to recognize and enhance their innate gifts while her skills and inspirational messages make Deborah a widely sought after Keynote Speaker.

———————————————

Deborah Johnson
Ontario, Canada
www.deborahjohnson.ca
deborah@deborahjohnson.ca